M000190858

HARUKI MURAKAMI GOES TO MEET HAYAO KAWAI

Haruki Murakami
Goes to Meet
Hayao Kawai

Translated from the Japanese
by Christopher Stephens

DAIMON

With special thanks to Hayao Kawai and Haruki Murakami for sharing
their reflections, and to Toshio Kawai, Hiromi Morikawa, Akemi
Watanabe, Blue Kim, Deanne Bosak and unnamed others for their
invaluable contributions to the realization of this project

murakami haruki, kawai hayao ni ai ni iku
by Hayao Kawai and Haruki Murakami
© 1996 by Kayoko Kawai and Haruki Murakami
First published 1996 by Iwanami Shoten, Publishers, Tokyo.

Photograph of the authors: July 2003 at Granvia Kyoto Hotel,
Photo: Kenji Sugano
© Shinchosha Publishing Co., Ltd., Tokyo, reproduced by permission.

This English edition, translated by Christopher Stephens
and edited by Robert Hinshaw, published 2016
by Daimon Verlag, Einsiedeln
by arrangement with the proprietors c/o Iwanami Shoten,
Publishers, Tokyo.

ISBN 978-3-85630-764-6

Cover image: "Grand old tree", © Daimon Verlag

Contents

Preface

The conversation comprising this book took place between two of Japan's foremost contemporary cultural spokespersons. While their extended talk took place at a particular location at a particular moment in history, much of the content is timeless and universal.

Hayao Kawai (1928-2007), designated a 'Person of Cultural Merit' and Minister of Culture for Japan from 2002 until his death five years later, originally studied mathematics and later trained to become a Jungian psychoanalyst and sandplay therapist in Zürich. He wrote some 20 books during his long life in the service of his country and humanity (for a brief biography and a listing of his works, see the website of the Hayao Kawai Foundation at www.kawaihayao.jp).

Haruki Murakami (1949-), after some years of running a jazz café with his wife, began dedicating himself to writing at the age of 30 and, in the course of the ensuing decades blossomed into one of the premier writers of his generation. His *oeuvre* includes reportage and short stories, and his genre-defying novels, including *The Wind-up Bird Chronicle, Norwegian Wood* and *1Q84,* are as well known in the West and other parts of the world as they are in Japan (for biographical information and a complete listing of his written works, see the website of Haruki Murakami at www.harukimurakami.com).

The two men first met, not insignificantly, in the United States in 1994. There was an instant mutual sympathy which led to Murakami later seeking out Kawai when both had resettled in their home country. The transcript of the two-day conversation that took place in November of 1995 forms the basis of this book.

I had the good fortune of encountering Hayao Kawai over the years at the Eranos Conferences* in Ascona, Ticino, where he was an honored and impressive guest speaker several times during the 1980s. As we came to know one another better, he became a Daimon author and we began publishing some of his writings in German and English, including a collection of his Eranos lectures**.

In an interview conducted at the International Jungian Congress in Barcelona in 2004, Kawai bubbled with energy as he detailed his life story, including his initial bold foray outside of Japan

---

* see www.eranosfoundation.org/history.htm
** Kawai, Hayao, *Dreams, Myths and Fairy Tales in Japan,* Daimon, Einsiedeln, 1995

to Los Angeles on a Fulbright Scholarship to study the Rorschach Projective Test with pioneer Bruno Klopfer. It was Professor Klopfer who first introduced him to Jungian thought and eventually analysis, and helped guide him to Zürich, where he trained to become a Jungian analyst and learned sandplay therapy from its originator, Dora Kalff.

He went on to introduce Jungian Psychology and sandplay in his home country, wrote numerous books and became a well-known public figure, culminating in his becoming President of the International Association of Sandplay Therapy and Japan's Minister of Culture in 2002.

By his own account, he was not particularly well-disposed towards traditional Japanese culture, and in his official work as Minister, he applied his knowledge and ever-developing Jungian-influenced world-view to the problems that were facing his Japan at the time. This included traveling around the country to the smallest of villages and encouraging his fellow citizens to *play* in whatever ways suited them in the face of their often depressive circumstances. He set an example himself by playing his flute for them and would also tell stories and laugh frequently, just as he would with a depressed client.*

---

* This interview was published in *IAAP Newsletter 25*, 2005, edited by Patricia Skar, International Association for Analytical Psychology, Zürich, pp. 59ff. It is also accessible on the website of Daimon Verlag: www.daimon.ch

Unbeknownst to us both, this daylong conversation in Barcelona was to be our last face-to-face encounter. He suffered a stroke, to which he eventually succumbed, taking many yet-to-be-written books and ideas to his grave.

Not long thereafter, Haruki Murakami's interest in C.G. Jung led him to visit Küsnacht and the Jung Institute with his wife Yoko in 2008, accompanied by the Japanese Ambassador to Switzerland and his wife. In the course of a long day arranged by Daniel Baumann that included an afternoon at Jung's Bollingen tower, Murakami told me of his first encounter in Boston with Kawai, and their ensuing friendship. He described seeking out his much-admired compatriot after they were both back in Japan, and their lengthy conversation comparing their histories, impressions of Japan from abroad, American and Japanese attitudes, how and why they each write, their views on relationship and the attitudes of young people: in short, their world-views and sources of meaning in their respective lives.

When he mentioned that a transcript of this conversation had been published in Japanese some years before, I was immediately interested and asked if there might be a version available in English or German, which there sadly was not. However in this moment, the idea of a possible future publication in English was born. Due to complicated copyright circumstances, discussions with regard to a potential English-language translation and publication were to continue for several years, but finally in mid-2016, all hurdles were cleared and it became possible for this project to be realized.

With the help of Toshio Kawai (son of Hayao, and himself a Jungian analyst in Kobe), an excellent translator was found in the person of Christopher Stephens, and work on the project commenced, with the ambitious goal of having it completed in time for the first-ever international Jungian Congress in Kyoto.

And thus it now becomes possible to introduce to an English-language readership this lively and relevant conversation between two acutely sensitive and perceptive men of their time.

– Robert Hinshaw
Editor, English Edition

Foreword

While I was living in the U.S., I had a chance to talk with Hayao Kawai on a few occasions. When you live abroad, the opportunity to meet someone you wouldn't normally meet in Japan sometimes arises. But at that time, I was writing a very long novel called *The Wind-Up Bird Chronicle,* and I was almost completely lost in the thick fog of the narrative. My story (and I) was definitely headed in some direction, but I had no idea where it was going. All kinds of different things were intricately entwined and there was no easy way to sort them out. On top of that, there were places where reality and fiction were jumbled together in dim disarray. It was like a closet full of stuff that hadn't been cleaned for about three years.

But when I spoke face-to-face with Kawai (even though I said almost nothing about the novel), I had the marvelous, gentle sensation that the irritation in my mind was abating. It might be an exaggeration to say that I was 'healed,' but I could certainly breathe easier. It might sound strange, but Hayao Kawai is an amazing person. I started to understand why he has so many passionate fans or believers – I know several myself.

The thing that always impresses me about talking with Kawai is that he never tries to influence you with his ideas. He pays close attention to what you're saying without interrupting the spontaneous flow of your thoughts. Instead, he follows you and slowly alters his position. For example, when he found out that I was working on a novel, Kawai avoided any statements that had the potential to lead me (or my work) in a given direction. Then he started to talk about things that were almost totally unrelated. Ultimately, however, this led me to a few natural conduits of thought and allowed me to decide which way to go. Or at least, that's how it seemed to me.

Without my knowing it, he had provided me with a great deal of encouragement. Since I tend to be a practical person rather than a theorist and I'm also a novelist, I was often persuaded by Kawai's attitude as a professional practitioner. In talking with him, I was constantly impressed by how fast he could switch from one mode of thought to another and by how sharply he concentrated on a particular subject.

But this time when I met him, I had finished the novel and there weren't any more restricted areas that I was trying to avoid. As the title suggests, I took the bullet train to Kawai's home area of Kyoto, and over two nights, we talked to our heart's content about all of the things we hadn't talked about before. The format wasn't like a formal dialogue. As we chatted, drank beer, ate delicious food, and told stupid jokes (as I recall there was a lot of laughter), we talked about whatever popped into our heads. I made a conscious effort to avoid difficult words – of course, I don't really know that many to start with, but anyway.

We didn't plan to talk about certain subjects in advance, and we didn't really revise the text after the conversations had been transcribed. We wanted to avoid impeding the natural flow. When we wanted to talk about something in greater detail or provide more explanation, we added footnotes. To be honest, it is extremely rare for me, as someone who is an innately bad speaker, to spontaneously express myself as succinctly as this. It's kind of miraculous. I'm sure that this is because Kawai is such a gifted listener.

At key points in the conversations, an editor from the Iwanami Shoten publishing company added a word or two. And for some of the time, my wife (she said she wanted to go to Kyoto, so I took her along) and Professor Jay Rubin of Harvard University, who was visiting Japan, joined us as guests. But to make the conversation flow more smoothly, we only included the things Kawai and I said in this book.

I thought about various titles for the book, but in the end I couldn't come up with anything better than *Haruki Murakami Goes to Meet Hayao Kawai*. It's simple and to the point – I think. Somehow it seems like the beginning of a story.

– Haruki Murakami

The First Night: How Do Stories Heal People?

1. The Meaning of Commitment

Murakami: *I just returned to Japan a few months ago after living in America for about four-and-a-half years. The thing that made the biggest impression on me after I came back was that various issues that I had been dealing with in my mind before I left suddenly seemed very different.*

For example, when I was in Japan, I was intensely motivated to be an individual. What I mean by that is, I did whatever I could to avoid things like societies, groups, organizations, and rules. I never worked a regular job after graduating from university, I made my own living as a writer, and I found the literary world exhausting. In the end, I simply wrote novels alone.

I spent about three years in Europe, came back to Japan for a year, and then after I had been in America for a little over three years, everything turned around. I started to feel like I should give more thought to my own sense of social responsibility.

Particularly after I went to America, I started

to feel that there was no longer any need to escape from things as an individual. Since we have no other choice but to live as individuals, that desire started to seem meaningless.

Kawai: That's interesting. Here's something I often say to people working in education. At schools these days, it's common to see big signs in the classroom saying things like, "Value individuality!" or "Foster

---

Murakami: *On the Question of Commitment*

The reason I focused primarily on detachment at the beginning of my career as a novelist wasn't simply that I wanted to depict the absence of commitment in a wider context, but rather that by steadily pursuing aspects of personal detachment, I felt it would be possible to dispense with various external values (for the most part, this was related to what is generally referred to as "novelistic values"), and by doing so, I could clearly determine my own position.

On a personal level, this was also a period in which I was increasingly thinking, "Just leave me alone!" (This had to do with my original personality as well as a few other, more concrete reasons.)

But at some point in the course of writing about this, my feelings slowly began to change. One of the biggest reasons was that I went to live abroad for quite an extended period. Though neither particularly good nor bad, the experience of being forced to adopt a more earnest viewpoint in everyday life played a significant part in this change. There were of course factors too, such as getting older, and learning to deal with and cure various aspects of myself.

*Editor's note: At various points in the protocol, the protagonists have added explanatory remarks that are set in smaller type and appear at the bottom of the respective page.

individuality!" When I tell people there isn't anything like that in America, they're really taken aback.

They ask me, "Isn't individuality important in America?" And I tell them, "That kind of thing is taken for granted, so there's no need to go out of your way to write it down."

If a school principal in Japan said, "Value individuality!", everybody would just say, "Huh?" So instead they say, "Let's foster individuality together!" And before you know it, everyone is united in a single group. That tells you how difficult

---

Kawai: On Commitment

As I read Murakami's comment, I was reminded of something. After I returned from Switzerland to Japan in 1965, I half-jokingly referred to what I had learned at the C.G. Jung Institute as the "Three Cs": complex, constellation, and commitment. Here, I'll omit the first two and focus on the last.

It is necessary for an analyst to adopt a neutral stance, and this has parallels with a detached attitude. But by undergoing analysis myself, I began to realize how committed analysts are to their work. Without commitment, it would be impossible to move forward with psychoanalytic therapy. So I learned to embrace the same attitude. It should be said, though, that this commitment is not the regular sort of "I'm ready for anything!" or "I'll do my best!", but something that can have the appearance of detachment. In a word, it's a quiet, deep sense of commitment.

If today's young people learned to understand this quiet sense of commitment, I think it would lead to a strong youth movement. It is necessary for them to learn how to commit with their entire beings, not just their minds.

it is for Japanese people to understand the meaning of individuality.

I read something interesting the other day. It was an introduction to a school that was trying to internationalize its curriculum based on the idea that Japanese schools need to become more international. There was a section in the text about moral education and it said that the expression '*sumimasen*' [excuse me] was extremely important. It also said that it was very important to use this phrase even when you hadn't done anything wrong. The teachers say the same thing. They don't teach anything about how there are other cultures where people don't say "excuse me" unless they do something wrong. In morals class, all they say is that the phrase is very important for smoothing out human relations.

It seems to be very difficult for Japanese people to understand the meaning of individuality through experience.

Murakami: *Recently, I've also been thinking a lot about 'commitment.' For instance, even when I'm writing a novel, commitment has become a very important thing for me. But it used to be that 'detachment' was the important thing.*

Kawai: Right, right, I understand.

Murakami: *At some point or other, it gradually started to change. I think moving to another country* *had a lot to do with it. But then the big question becomes, What exactly should you commit to?*

While I was in America, I felt like I had given a lot of thought to things like what I should commit to and what I should do in the future. But in the end, once I got back to Japan, I had no idea what to commit to. It was a really big problem. Then I realized that there aren't any real rules in Japan about committing yourself.

Kawai: I think you're right. That's why you're likely to be ostracized if you're not careful and commit to something in the Western sense of the word.

Murakami: *Yes, or you also run the risk of being dragged slowly through a bottomless swamp.*

Thinking back on it now, the question of what to commit to became a big one for me around the time of the student protests in 1968 and '69. It wasn't like I had any clear political will at the time. And when you adopt a methodology without any clear notion of how to commit to something, you end up with very few options. I think that's what made everything so tragic.

In the end, that was an era of commitment for people of my generation. But it was smashed to pieces and in the blink of an eye, we had moved into a period of detachment. That's not only true for me; I think it's true for my entire generation.

Kawai: Young people today also have a very strong sense of detachment. So much so that they seem to believe that the ones who do commit to something are essentially fools. They seem to think that being detached is cool or fashionable.

Murakami: *But then in 1995, the Aum incident [a sarin gas attack on the Tokyo subway by a cult group called Aum Shinrikyo] and that big earthquake [the Great Hanshin-Awaji Earthquake] happened. Those events were closely related to the question of commitment.*

Murakami: *The Problem of Relating to the Outside World in Japan*

When I returned to Japan, I was faced with the problem of how to deal with the outside world. I gave this a lot of thought, but it was a difficult problem. I tried a few concrete things, but it was hard to find an approach that was right for me.

After giving it more thought, however, I realized that the problem was very similar to the problems I had faced in 1968. I had felt and thought the same kind of things at that time. And I had run into the same kind of wall. This made me think I had come full circle.

In the end, I arrived at the simple conclusion that the most effective way for me to deal with the outside world was through the act of writing. At the same time, it was clear that this was not enough. There were still many hardships I had to endure. There was no easy answer, especially since in a sense I had to revamp myself as a person.

One thing for sure is that the extended project I'm currently working on has provided me with some hints about a possible answer.

Kawai: Yes, they prompted a really strong reaction. Young people who were normally very detached suddenly became very committed.

An unexpectedly large number of young volunteers came to Kobe. I think that many Japanese people had a latent desire to commit to something, but it just hadn't surfaced yet. Then when the earthquake and the Aum thing happened, it suddenly emerged.

Murakami: *Both of those were events that tested the limits of our imagination. When those unusual situations arose, they triggered a sense of commitment for the first time.*

Kawai: I really need to do some more research, but I'd be interested to see how young Japanese people's volunteer activities after the earthquake differ or resemble those in America and other countries. In Japan, once people start to seriously commit themselves to something, they have a way of clinging to each other – it's like one big lump.

Murakami: *That's definitely what happened during the student movement.*

Kawai: That's why during that period I would often tease students by saying, "It might seem like you guys are doing something new, but the basic makeup of what you're doing and the way you're forming groups is very, very old." That was the funny thing about it.

When they all gathered together, if one person was only offering a little support, the others would say, "Hey, you're not being a *team player*!" In other words, there was no place for individual freedom. The ones that committed by clinging to the whole were the good guys, and the ones that did things according to their own individual ideas were heretics.

But people who commit to something in the West, commit as individuals. The way it works there is they come when they come, and when they don't, they don't.

Murakami: *Even though the people who volunteer have a variety of personal situations, if some of them come three times a week and some of them only come once, there's sure to be someone among the ones who come three times a week that starts to get arrogant about it.*

Kawai: Yes, there's always someone like that.

2. The Hanshin Earthquake and Emotional Trauma

Murakami: *Is there a lot of counseling going on in Kobe?*

Kawai: Yes, quite a lot. That's very different from the way it was in the past. They've also set up a helpline, and contrary to expectations, a large number of people have been using it. That's also different from the way it was in the past.

Another notable thing is – as I predicted from the start – that there is less PTSD than there would have been in the West.

Murakami: *Can you explain a bit more about PTSD?*

Kawai: Post-traumatic stress disorder refers to a condition that is manifested suddenly some time after a person who has experienced a terrible shock has begun to put their life back together. It's quite widespread in America. I have a friend who lives in Northridge, so after the earthquake happened there, he told me a lot about PTSD. Of course, there are a certain number of cases in Japan too, but rather than experiencing the shock as an individual, Japanese people experience it as a group. Here, it takes the form of domestic quarrels, but very few people display actual symptoms of neurosis.

At first, this seemed slightly encouraging, but there is a positive and negative side to it. In effect, the fact that so few people exhibit these types of symptoms suggests that they do not have the ability to face the anguish on their own.

This is somewhat off topic, but one of the most difficult types of people we meet as therapists are people who don't display any particular kind of symptom. For example, when someone tells us they have an anxiety disorder, we can clearly see that they are suffering a great deal of anxiety, so we know how to deal with them. On the other hand, when someone comes to us who doesn't seem to be suffering that much pain, but for some reason or another things are not going well, we have no way of knowing if things are good or bad just by looking at them.

But somehow you have the sense that people around them are also having trouble. If there is some sort of symptom – for example, if they suddenly do something wrong or cause some kind of problem – it's possible to diagnose them. But when we deal with a person in a situation in which everyone is having trouble, we say that they don't have the ability to formulate any symptoms.

Murakami: *In other words, they can't process or give form to the injuries or trauma that they have experienced.*

Kawai: Right. Generally, people try to process things in their own way, but when that fails, some type of symptom emerges. However in these cases, because the person can't process the experience and it's something they share with the people around them, they say things to each other like, "Hey, you have to be a little bit stronger."

Murakami: *Isn't that connected to their sense of responsibility?*

Kawai: Exactly. There are two types of responsibility: individual responsibility and collective responsibility. In Japan, we have collective or local responsibility. So when the earthquake happened in Kobe, the city as a whole had to deal with it.

Kawai: The Earthquake and Mental Health Care

When the earthquake happened, I quickly began to think about mental health care. Many Japanese people are terrible at verbalizing their feelings, and since there were people who were dealing with the situation as a whole, I wasn't sure if it was a good idea for therapists to immediately go out to the stricken area. So I started a helpline at the Japanese Society of Certified Clinical Psychologists, and

But in the West everything is rooted in personal responsibility, so people who find it hard to deal with these situations end up becoming neurotic.

Murakami: *But that also means that the people who are able to surmount these difficulties grow stronger.*

Kawai: Right. After attending some conferences on sandplay therapy in America, I realized that there are some very unfortunate situations there – cases that are unlike anything we've seen in Japan so far. For example, a father runs off and leaves his kids behind. Then the mother also abandons the kids to marry her new boyfriend. Now the kids are all alone in the world, so they go to live with people who are ostensibly their parents, but in reality they aren't related by blood. There are also cases where a couple gets divorced, the children stay with the father, and then he marries a new woman. But then he suddenly leaves and the woman marries a new man, so the kids end up living with parents who are completely unrelated to them.

In this sort of situation, some children completely stop talking, and start running wild and

---

decided that if there were a big response, I would arrange for direct consultations.

Since there were in fact more calls than I had expected, a number of clinical psychologists were sent out to the area. This allowed us to provide assistance, though the total number of PTSD cases was, as I had originally predicted, much lower than it would have been in the West.

causing havoc. Despite this, they actually do recover – that shows you how strong they are.

In Japan, some people just cry and complain. They say things like, "Why am I the only unlucky one?" It's ultimately very difficult for them to accept that they can only surmount their problems on their own. After all, responsibility in this society lies with everyone. Their attitude is, "Please, do something to ease my pain!" That makes it difficult for them to recover.

Kawai: What is Sandplay Therapy?

Sandplay therapy is a psychological treatment that was developed by the Swiss therapist Dora Kalff. The patient is asked to approach a sandbox and create a work using a variety of miniature objects. This expressive activity is intended to trigger the person's self-healing power and to cure them.

After I introduced the technique in Japan in 1965, it spread rapidly and I later succeeded Kalff as the president of the Japan Association of Sandplay Therapy. I also make frequent trips to foreign countries to provide instruction in sandplay therapy.

3. Words or Images?

Murakami: *When you watch Americans doing sandplay, does it definitely seem to have a healing effect?*

Kawai: Yes, it's very clear. It's quite a remarkable thing.

Murakami: *Does it have a more logical form than the type of recovery you see in Japanese people?*

Kawai: No, not necessarily. You can't really say it's logical because it's such a deep thing. Each person unearths their own experiences. And although the wounds they suffer in the process might also be deep, there is a great healing power that emerges from this pain.

In Japan, we usually lend someone a helping hand before the wound becomes too deep, so there aren't that many severe cases. In America, they use an approach that is so radical that it probably wouldn't work for Japanese people, but that really works for them.

Since sandplay is rooted in an imaginary world, it's very easy for Japanese people to understand it; I think that's why it's become so widespread here. The method has shown good results in Europe, where it was originally developed, and I'm trying to make it more popular in America.

In America, standard psychotherapy, particularly present-day techniques, is considered to be 'scientific.' What this means is, let's say a person has the feeling that they have something stuck in their throat and they can't eat anything. When something seems to be stuck in a person's throat and they find it difficult to even drink water, despite the fact that there is nothing wrong with them medically, in American psychotherapy they investigate the cause

---

Kawai: Japanese People and Sandplay

Doing sandplay and writing stories is more or less the same thing, except that sandplay is nonverbal. Japanese people tend to be better at this sort of thing, which in part explains why sandplay therapy has become so widespread in Japan.

In Western sandplay, after the person creates a work, they explain what they've made in words by saying things like, "This is me," "This stone is my father," and "This tree is my mother." Distancing themselves from language seems to be difficult.

On the other hand, Japanese people arrange the objects without any explanation based on a vague feeling or just because something seems interesting. This results in profound expressions.

and solve the problem by relying solely on words. They ask the person things like, "What exactly is it that's stuck in your throat?", or "Isn't there something that you have been avoiding talking about?"

In Japan, however, we would never ask the person anything in that kind of situation. If we say anything, it's something like, "Oh, that sounds tough" or "Would you like to try some sandplay?" And then, before they know it, the lump in their throat is gone.

Recently, I've adopted a more and more radical approach. When someone comes to me for a consultation, I no longer try to analyze them. In the past, I could figure out quite a lot by analyzing a person, but these days I don't try to figure anything out. I don't do anything, I just say things like, "I see." But somehow that seems to be more effective.

This is something I try to stress with Americans. It's wrong to think that someone can't be cured without analyzing and verbalizing everything. In fact, if you're not careful, analytic methods based on language can make the wound deeper.

For example, let's say someone said, "There's something stuck in my throat," and you said, "You must have something you want to say. Don't hold back, just come out and say it," and they replied, "Actually, I want to kill my father." By coming out and saying this, they create more pain. Even though they had never consciously thought about it, when they realize that they intended to kill their father, it causes them pain.

If you used the sandplay method instead, their feelings would emerge symbolically in the sandbox. The sandbox occupies an intermediate point between total analysis and a nonverbal treatment. I'd like to see Western people use this approach too, so I'm doing my best to make it more well known.

Linguistic analysis is easy to use in cases when the problem lies near the level of normal consciousness. But when the problem is deeply rooted, even

---

Kawai: On Verbalization

My stance is sometimes misinterpreted as being diametrically opposed to verbalization. This is not the case. I am opposed to psychotherapy that centers on verbalizing and to the idea of a psychotherapist treating someone solely by 'interpreting' what they say. This is due to the fact that when they 'interpret' something, the therapist often relies on words to contextualize the client based on the therapist's own theories (many of which are Western in origin).

Whereas, I believe in providing treatment based on images derived from sandplay, dreams, etc. The therapist should attempt to internally verbalize things as accurately as possible, and when necessary (this is the difficult part) convey them to the client.

However, it is extremely difficult to verbalize my approach in a widely accessible form, and I'm afraid I have failed at doing this in the past. I have written many books, but I have primarily focused on things that are easily understandable.

In books like *The Wind-Up Bird Chronicle*, Murakami seems to be writing about things that are closely related to what I'm doing in my work. For this, I am deeply grateful.

when you try to use words to analyze the person, the pain only grows worse, and in some cases, it does not help them at all. So in my view, it's important to alter your approach according to the problem.

Murakami: *Are there cases when it proves to be absolutely impossible to uncover the problem – for example, a person who, despite having a problem, tries to keep it hidden?*

Kawai: It would be pretty amazing for a person to realize that they had a problem and intentionally try to hide it. We always tell people that if they don't want to say something, they don't have to. Some people do their utmost to avoid saying something for three years or so, and that ends up curing them.

Murakami: *That's really something.*

Kawai: Yes, especially since we also realize that they're doing their best to avoid talking about it. Some people eventually say that at the end, and other people say things like, "I finally succeeded in not talking about it."

4. Answering Logically vs. Answering Compassionately

Murakami: *I've got a thing about newspaper advice columns; I read them constantly when I was in America. They're absolutely fascinating. First of all, the type of questions people ask is completely different from the ones they ask in Japan. The way they answer or respond to the questions is also different. And the type of people who give the answers is different too. In Japanese advice columns, the people who give the answers are so-called 'intellectuals,' but the columnists in America are advice specialists or people who have been offering advice for decades, and they're syndicated throughout the country. That's why the answers are so different from the ones in Japanese advice columns.*

Kawai: That's an area that would really merit a comparative study.

Murakami: *A while back there was an interesting one about a housewife who cleaned the house in the nude. After seeing her husband and children off in the morning, she'd take off all her clothes and start cleaning. But one day a man broke inside her house and raped her. She had always really enjoyed cleaning in the nude, but after she was raped her outlook on life changed. She could only see the world in negative terms, so she wrote in to ask what she could do. This is the kind of question that you would never get in Japan.*

The columnist was a woman and she replied that although she understood that it was probably very pleasant to clean house in the nude, it defied common sense because there was a potential that a man could break in and rape her, and that made it a dangerous thing to do.

This response sparked a huge backlash. A succession of housewives wrote in to say that they also cleaned house in the nude. The columnist was forced to apologize. She said that she hadn't realized that so many housewives cleaned house in the nude, and that she had made a mistake. And the interesting thing was that she wrote a follow-up saying that if there were that many people doing it, we should make an effort to protect their rights.

When American people feel that a columnist's response isn't quite right, they write in from all over the country. This would never happen in Japan.

Kawai: No, it wouldn't. In fact, there are plenty of questions in Japanese advice columns that don't really seem to have come from real people. When they're short on letters, the columnist just makes something up. Still, lots of people do enjoy reading these columns.

Murakami: *The replies in Japanese advice columns either agree with the person or encourage them to do something. It seems like the people who write in aren't actually looking for a logical answer like do this or do that.*

Kawai: If the columnist answered logically, people would say, "He doesn't understand anything about human nature" or "That's easy for her to say because she doesn't know how it feels."

5. Things That Surprised Me
after Becoming a Novelist

Murakami: *When I became a novelist, there weren't any novelists I wanted to emulate in terms of lifestyle. The first thing I set out to do was to behave in ways that were the complete opposite of what had been seen as the normal writer's lifestyle. I decided to get up early in the morning, go to bed early at night, and build up my physical strength by exercising. I also decided to avoid the literary world, and never to write any novels on commission. After resolving these minor details, I started to work.*

Everything seemed to go pretty well. But after working as a writer for a long time, I reached an impasse in this society. That was the situation I found myself in prior to leaving Japan.

I thought that being a novelist was an extremely personal act. It seemed like a writer's life meant writing whatever you wanted to, going out and selling it, and getting paid in return. There wasn't any need to deal with anyone else. But as it turned out, it isn't really like that. The literary world is a microcosm of Japanese society. I didn't realize that until I became a novelist. And when I did, it seemed very surprising and strange.

Writing novels in a place like Japan became very painful for me. The reality was that there were all kinds of little chores and lots of complicated things that had to be done, and it gradually became more and more difficult to concentrate on my work. Anyway, I decided I wanted to go to another country and write, and until recently I was living in America. As I mentioned earlier, when you live in a completely different place for two or three years, your way of thinking and looking at things changes little by little.

Then for some reason or other, after I finished writing The Wind-Up Bird Chronicle, *I decided it was time to head back to Japan. At the end, I really wanted to go back. It wasn't like I was feeling*

Murakami: *On Novelists*

Perhaps my remark about trying to do the complete opposite of the writer's lifestyle was overly simplistic and reckless. However, there is no doubt that at that time in my career, I wanted to rebel against the literary world. Frankly speaking, I was quite impudent. I was young and defiant. But this was something I needed to do. With almost nothing at my disposal, I was forced to use my hands to clear the way and construct my own literary style and lifestyle.

The lifestyle that I developed then remains intact today, some 20 years later, and in a way, it has become even more extreme than it was at that time. But I'm not as rebellious as I was then. For one thing, I've firmly established my style over the years, and for another, there isn't anything I want particularly nostalgic or that there was a cultural revival going on here; I just felt that the place I belonged as a novelist was Japan.

Ultimately, writing in Japanese means that your thought system is Japanese. And since Japanese was created in Japan, the language is inseparable from the country. In any case, what really struck home with me was that I couldn't write novels or stories in English.

Kawai: Sure, writing a short essay or something in English might be okay, but writing a novel would be out of the question.

Murakami: *There are some people who defected from their own country and wrote novels in a foreign language – for example, writers from South America who went to America and wrote in English. Nabokov and Conrad both wrote novels in their second language. And recently there are people like the poet*

---

to rebel against or anything that deserves to be rebelled against. Since I began writing, the Japanese literary world has changed quite a lot. Meaningless rules in the industry that once governed how things should be have disappeared, and the system is much more open than it was. The public consensus about what constitutes literature is no longer as defined as it once was. I see these as positive developments.

Despite the systematic changes, I don't think that what Kawai referred to as "sticky human relations" will ever change, no matter how much time passes, so the only option is to reconcile yourself to the situation.

Joseph Brodsky. But I decided I had to come back to Japan and write in Japanese.

Kawai: That's because the linguistic structure of Japanese is completely different from English and other European languages. And more than that,

---

Kawai: On Rebellion

I was struck by Murakami's comment that there isn't anything left to rebel against. I think this view is shared by many young people today.

In my youth, and later in Murakami's youth, it was easy for young people to find something to rebel against. All you had to do was take an 'anti-establishment' view of the existing 'establishment.' But under current conditions, the establishment doesn't have as clear a form as it once did, and even if you committed yourself to an anti-establishment movement, people now realize how hollow the results tend to be.

On the other hand, the fundamental structures remain largely unchanged. The approach of defining the establishment and thinking in terms of its opposite is essentially part of the establishment now. So no matter how intense the commitment might seem on the surface, it lacks depth, and eventually weakens and fades.

As an example of what today's youth might do, I would suggest the approach that Murakami has taken. Rather than rebelling against the establishment, I would recommend using "[your] own hands to clear the way and construct a literary style and lifestyle." This will produce new results. Instead of a schematically conceived commitment to rebellion, which is limited to the mind and fades like fireworks, it is important to make a full-body commitment to creating your own style. This will in turn lead to the creation of your own 'work.'

When I say 'work,' I am not referring to a work of art, but to the fact that the way a person lives can in itself the thinking pattern is different. I think the fact that, as you mentioned at the outset, you started considering what it meant to be an individual and decided to leave Japan for a while and write in Japanese is a highly significant thing. But in terms of moving forward with your work, I don't think there was any other choice but to come back to Japan and write in Japanese.

Murakami: *Yes, until that point I couldn't stand the Japanese that was being used in Japanese novels. There was something really cloying about pure literature and I-novels [a Japanese genre of confessional fiction written in the first person] that didn't fully relativize the self (or ego). At the time, I found this deeply distasteful, and I tried to get as far away from it as I could. But now it finally seems as if the use of language in Japanese literature is changing a little.*

---

be a work. In this regard, I have great hopes for today's youth. By avoiding a rebellious style and coming up with your own personal style, you can get to the heart of the existing society and culture, and help generate a movement in the process. When this movement emerges, and adults are applauding it as a further strengthening of their own 'establishment,' they will be staggered to discover the 'violence' that is contained within it. Doesn't this seem like a feasible approach?

Murakami: *Japanese Language and Literature in Foreign Countries*

I am incredibly bad at teaching, and have constantly avoided it, but while I was in America, I felt obliged to teach classes at two universities (Princeton and Tufts) that had

Young people write differently today. I think this is a very important transition. And of course, changes in linguistic systems and thought systems influence each other. One reason I wanted to come back was that it seemed that as part of this trend, there was more potential for writing in Japanese.

Another reason was that in the process of talking and dealing with American writers, I felt that I couldn't completely convey my intentions in English. Of course, part of that had to do with my own linguistic inadequacy, but there was more to it than that. Ultimately, I couldn't convey my way of approaching and experiencing the novel. There was an unbridgeable gap in my basic understanding of literature and at first that seemed refreshing, but after a while my sense of frustration grew stronger.

---

been very kind to me. I decided to teach Japanese novels. Or more accurately, I was provided with a venue to discuss things with the students – thinking back on it now, that was really all I did.

As texts, I chose books by 'third-generation writers' of the postwar era. This was because in recent years I had gradually started to become interested in their work. Also, during my stay in America, I had made a concentrated effort to read a lot of Japanese novels. Until that point, I had never attempted to systematically read them, so that was a completely new experience for me. Though I couldn't do much as a teacher (I'm just not cut out for it), the experience was beneficial.

Reading Japanese novels in a foreign country was a very valuable linguistic experience. I developed the ability to see the strengths, functions, and uses of Japanese within the structure of the novel from a wide-ranging perspective.

That was quite difficult for me, but that was another reason I decided it was about time to head back.

Another thing was that I've been doing translation for a long time, and I always had the feeling that I was being changed by changing one language into another. But this feeling gradually decreased. Recently, when I translate something, there is less dynamism involved in learning something as a writer.

By converting English – with its wholly different physiology, rhythm, and sensibility – into Japanese, I had the feeling that I was creating something inside of me. But over time that feeling faded. I'm not sure what sort of effect this might have overall; it's something that I'm still thinking about.

6. The Japanese Individual
and the Underlying Threads of History

Kawai: In Japan, it's very difficult to understand the meaning of 'individual' in the Western sense of the word.

Murakami: *That's true.*

Kawai: For example, you mentioned the I-novel earlier, and even though Japanese writers use the word 'I,' it's something completely different from what is referred to as the 'ego' in the West.

In order to really deal with the subject of the individual, you have to actually go to the West. You must have had a lot of trouble translating things from the West into Japanese and adequately conveying the concept of the individual to the Japanese reader. I imagine that in the past this was a very important concern for you, but probably not so much anymore.

Sorry to be so presumptuous, but that's the way it seems to me. I also love individualism, am fond of the West, and lived there too, but lately I have the sense that the English word 'individual' is different from the Japanese individual, which is the subject we're trying to deal with here.

For example, if you really wanted to depict individuality in a novel, you wouldn't necessarily have to rely on Western individualism as a foundation. In fact, a Japanese writer would almost certainly stray from that foundation anyway, and their attempts to deal with the subject would be different.

That's also the sense I got from reading *The Wind-Up Bird Chronicle*. In a nutshell, it's about going down into a well. The main character goes down into the well, and the well leads to Khalkhyn Gol and other very deep places. If this was a Western individual, it would create a situation in which the reader is forced to consider the history of Khalkhyn Gol, so you'd never be able to get there via the well. The Western individual's way of thinking is based on accumulating ideas (first, there was a historical incident involving the Japanese in Khalkhyn Gol, then this and that happened, and finally, the atomic bombs were dropped) and adopting a viewpoint.

But the sense I had from reading your book was that Khalkhyn Gol is still going on – everything is still going on. Assuming that there are individuals who react in this way, I think they're different from the individuals normally associated with Western individualism.

Murakami: *It's hard to explain, but I had the sense that in order to capture the individual in Japan, the only choice was to deal with history.*

If you try to depict a present-day individual, someone living in our age, the definition of an individual in Japan becomes, as you suggest, extremely ambiguous. But somehow I felt that by bringing in the underlying threads of history, it would be easier to understand an individual living in Japan.

Kawai: As far as history goes, Western people tend to plot a series of events on a straight line to show that certain events occurred in a given month in a given year. But I think Japanese people see history as a mass of undefined things. For example, we are satisfied with a concept like 'ancestral tomb'; we don't feel any need to know each person's name or the order they came in. I think the key here is your emphasis on 'the underlying thread of history.' This element has the potential to help us see the Japanese individual from a new perspective.

7. The Depth of Linguistic Differences

Murakami: *Returning to the subject of translation, the most difficult thing about translating English into Japanese is the pronouns. It always seems to me that unless you can find a good way of dealing with the pronouns, the translation falls flat. Pronouns are in effect a means of defining the individual.*

After translating for over a decade, I gradually learned how to handle this kind of definition. Sometimes I still wonder if it's really okay to define things to this degree and ask myself how I ever got so used to doing this.

At the same time, these are not clearly defined concepts within me, they are obscure, ambiguous things.

For example, the past tense is constantly used in English, but saying that one thing happened *and then another thing* happened *in Japanese doesn't make for a good reading experience. So you have to switch to present tense at a suitable point, and here again, you start getting further and further away from the original language.*

Jay Rubin is translating The Wind-Up Bird Chronicle *right now and he sometimes calls me up to ask a question like, "Why is this part in the present tense?" or "Should I use the present tense in English, too?" I often explain, "No, don't worry about it. I just used the present to make it sound better."*

But he's an argumentative kind of guy, so he'll say things like, "But there must be more to it than that." And he's right, there is more to it. It's also important to increase the tension and establish a rhythm in the

---

Murakami: *On Translation*

Whenever I have some free time, I sit down at my desk and translate, and sometimes I ask myself why it is that I like translation so much. Even I don't really know why. The only thing I can say is that there is something about the process of reading a text in a foreign language, understanding it, and changing it into idiomatic Japanese, that is deeply attractive to me.

When I translate, I sometimes turn into an invisible man via the text. I have the sensation that I have entered another person's (i.e., the writer's) heart or mind. It's similar to quietly sneaking into a house when no one is home. Maybe this is because I am so interested in having this kind of relationship with the writer through the text. Needless to say, this is not something that is possible with just any writer or text. I can only have this relationship with something that seems special to me.

I think that in order to do a good translation, it's necessary to have a deep sense of emptiness and sympathy. Conversely, without these feelings, I can't translate well.

text as a whole. Then he might say, "So doesn't that mean that I should do the same thing in the English translation?" When he says something like that, I find myself at a loss.

Kawai: As you suggest, there is a strong tendency in Japanese to create a rhythm and tension through the sound of the language. But English is very different because there's such a strong emphasis on logical structure.

Murakami: *Right. For example, in English there is a subtle difference between a colon and a semicolon, but since this isn't true in Japanese, we use something else instead.*

Kawai: When something seems overly assertive or strong, we add a particle like *ga* and waffle on for a while.

Murakami: *When I have to give a speech in English, I write a draft in English. If I wrote it in Japanese and then translated it into English, it wouldn't work. I would start losing track of what I was saying.*

Kawai: That's why I always write in English when I have to give a speech, too. If you try to turn something you thought up in Japanese into English, it becomes very difficult.

Murakami: *My books have been translated into English and I sometimes discuss them with American* *students, but I have the feeling that the translations don't quite match up. On the other hand, the students are impressed and interested in unexpected things. Asian readers, though, are usually pretty similar to Japanese readers.*

Kawai: Even if they read the books in English?

Murakami: *Yes, regardless of whether they read them in English or Chinese or Korean. The interesting*

Kawai: The Desire to Make a Speech in English

The first time I met Murakami at Princeton University in the U.S. (in the spring of 1994), I was actually reading *The Tale of Genji*. I'm embarrassed to admit it, but I had never read it before, so I concentrated on it throughout my two-month stay there. Unless I had taken advantage of that opportunity, it would have been difficult to make it through the entire book.

The fact that I read it abroad made it more meaningful. I read it as I was dealing with the way that contemporary Americans think and feel, so there was an even stronger contrast and I realized what a tremendous book it was. I was also impressed to find that it had lost none of its freshness. After finishing the book and thinking about how a Japanese woman had created something so amazing nearly 1,000 years ago, I became so excited I found it hard to sleep.

Some day I'd like to share this experience in English with a foreign audience. By doing that, I think I will be able to, as Murakami suggested, see *The Tale of Genji** from a different perspective.

* Hayao Kawai's book on Genji, *Murasaki-Mandala*, has not been published in English, but there is a German-language version: *Die Frauen um Prinz Genji, eine japanische Geschichte voller Weisheit*, translated by Irene Büchli, Daimon Verlag, Einsiedeln, 2003.

thing is they tend to be looking for detachment. In other words, they want to live differently from their society and their parents, and they read this sense of detachment into my novels. They seem to be very devoted to this pursuit.

A while ago I was interviewed by some Korean newspapers and magazines and most of the questions had to do with detachment. But as far as I'm concerned, this is a phase that I've already passed through, and to tell the truth, I'm not very interested in that subject anymore. I felt sorry that I couldn't really answer their questions, but...

Kawai: That's interesting. In the future, I imagine that detachment is going to be a very big issue in Korea and China. Family and household ties are extremely important there, so trying to detach yourself from them can be a life-threatening undertaking.

Murakami: *Do you think we might see a rise in mental and pathological problems as a result?*

Kawai: I'm sure there will be all kinds of problems.

On a slightly different topic, Korean people have become Westernized even faster than Japanese, and according to some Koreans, they have also become overly egocentric. They are apparently taking individualism too far, and only looking out for their own interests without giving any thought to society as a whole. Japanese people are unusual in the sense that even though we've been Westernized, we still give a surprising amount of thought to other people, so some people say that we should learn to be more individual.

This is not my personal view, but Koreans are said to lack individualism. Their identities are rooted in the family – you might say they have a family ego. This is different from Western individualism, in which people are constantly aware of the way in which they relate to each other as individuals, and the dangers that are involved in these relationships. In Korea, however, when they step outside the family ego, they really become egoistic, and that is apparently the problem.

Japanese people are different because we don't have a family ego. We have a field identity, and we use individual places as a foundation for our identity. Because of this fascinating characteristic, we approach our workplaces and homes as fields, and are able to function well in each situation.

Korean people who have discovered individualism in the truest sense of the word want to detach from their family. That requires a tremendous amount of drive. With this mind, it makes perfect sense that so many people detect a sense of detachment in your novels and are deeply affected by them.

8. Things Are Starting to Heat Up

Murakami: *We already talked a bit about problems like Aum and the earthquake, but I have the sense that Japanese society is on the verge of a huge transition in terms of emotional commitment. It seems to me that Japan has changed quite a lot over the last two or three years. I think this is another reason why I wanted to come back.*

Kawai: It's important for us to convey this feeling as best we can to younger people. Younger people today don't really understand commitment. They're often said to be unrealistic or apathetic, but university students are well aware of the fact that their predecessors' attempts to detach themselves from society in the 1960s ended in failure, so they find it hard to emulate them. At the same time, they have absolutely no idea what to commit to.

Murakami: *I have a strong feeling that we're going to see student protests again. Things are starting to heat up now and if they really reach a boiling point, I think even bigger changes are bound to follow.*

I was living in America when the Gulf War happened, and that was pretty hard. It was painfully clear that Japan's reasoning and the reasoning of the rest of the world did not mesh at all. I had no way of explaining the situation to American people. Since I understand the Japanese perspective in regard to not sending troops to the region, I wanted to explain it to them, but it was impossible.

There is no question that the Self-Defense Forces is an army. But despite the fact that Japan has an army, we can't send troops into combat because we renounced war in the 'Pacifist Constitution' [i.e., the

---

Murakami: *On the Gulf War*

As I mentioned in our conversation, I was in America at the time of the Gulf War, and I gave a great deal of thought to the meaning of that conflict. Then not long after the war had ended, I began writing an introspective text called, "What Exactly Did the Gulf War Mean to Japanese People?", without any particular plan to publish it. Roughly five years have passed, but I'm still not finished. It isn't that long; I just can't find a good way to end it. I think this is because the text hinges on the fact that Japan's postwar values have served very little purpose in the world, and also because this issue is closely connected to my own values and those of my entire generation. This makes it even more difficult to come to a conclusion. I've continued to think about it for the last five years.

Nobody seems to remember the Gulf War today, but to me it's like a little bone that remains stuck in the back of my throat. I understand what Kawai says about it being best to allow for contradictions, and I know that's the only thing we can do at this point, but at the same time, I'm still not completely satisfied.

postwar Constitution, which prevents Japan from using military force]. This is a total contradiction, and there's no way to explain it. That's what made me feel so mixed up.

This made me wonder about the causes my generation fought for at the end of the '60s. As I thought back on everything and asked myself what it all meant and whether in the end it wasn't just a hypocritical pursuit, I started to question the meaning of my own life. That in turn made it seem necessary to go back a couple of decades and take another look at what happened.

Kawai: On the Gulf War

I too am still considering the Gulf War. It's a problem without a simple answer. Though I did talk about allowing for contradictions, I also believe that we have yet to resolve the issue. In other words, while recognizing the contradictions, we have to find an answer by calmly searching for a *realistic* solution. At the same time, we must remain obsessively focused on the contradictions. We should identify and verbalize their existence and essence, and devise a way to eliminate them. However, there is no rush to find a solution. In the course of examining a problem, something that first appears to be a contradiction can morph into something that is free of contradiction when seen from a different perspective or in the context of a different dimension.

In that sense, there are lots of small bones stuck in my throat, and as I go on living, I wonder when I might be able to swallow them. The Gulf War is one of the larger bones. And it is important for Japanese people to involve themselves more deeply in this problem.

If I had been living in Japan, this never would have occurred to me. Even if I understood it logically, I don't think I could have ever felt it in such an acute way.

The 50th anniversary of the attack on Pearl Harbor was just after that. Since that was an event that happened before I was born, I couldn't understand it even if I tried, but it still raised a lot of questions. I had to find out what World War II meant to me, and this was also painful. But as I thought about all of these things (Pearl Harbor, Khalkhin Gol, etc.), I started to realize that there are many things like this dwelling inside of me.

I also realized that even though the war was over and everything had been rebuilt, nothing has essentially changed in Japanese society. That was one reason I decided to write about the Battle of Khalkhin Gol in The Wind-Up Bird Chronicle. *As I tried to retrace my life and figure out who I was, it inevitably forced me to take a closer look at society and history as a whole.*

I'm still searching for a suitable way of explaining Pearl Harbor and Japan's role in the war, but at this point I'm at a total loss. If I continue my search in a logical manner, I might eventually be able to make sense of what [Japanese politician] Ichiro Ozawa is getting at, but if I just continue on as I have been, everything will probably just get more confused.

Kawai: To be perfectly frank, Japan operates in a very devious way, so it would probably be best for the rest of the world to be a little more devious. (laughs)

They have to learn to adjust their level of deviousness, examine the harmful effects of deviousness more closely, and refine their way of operating in a devious way. Because Japanese people do devious things without ever saying that's what they're up to. Then when they meet with criticism, they go on the defensive.

If you rephrased the word 'devious' slightly, you might say that Japanese people are simply trying to maintain a logical consistency in regard to their philosophical and political positions. Human beings are deeply contradictory, so when we say something based on a viewpoint that contains a certain amount of inconsistency, it comes off as a devious act.

But when America condemns Japan's actions at Pearl Harbor, there is no room for contradictions. To allow such a thing would be a total indictment of the anti-war Constitution. At the same time, applying the logic of the Constitution to America's actions would also result in a total indictment. In a situation like this, the Japanese approach would be to say something like, "Well, we can probably have it both ways, right?" And that makes it possible to do something else with the money that was supposed to go toward the war. That's considered to be the best way of dealing with the situation.

However, it's extremely difficult to explain this philosophy of deviousness in English.

Murakami: *Yes, it's very difficult. It's difficult because it's something you can't really understand without experiencing it firsthand.*

But it seems to me that ultimately what led modern Japan to war was this kind of deviousness and ambiguity.

The type of refined deviousness that you're talking about would never have been effective unless the person actually realized they were being inconsistent.

Kawai: Absolutely.

Murakami: *But in practical terms, it would be impossible to do this, wouldn't it?*

Kawai: How do you mean?

Murakami: *Regardless of how it might be for individual people, it would be pretty difficult for Japan as a whole to admit that it was devious, and to attempt to move forward while recognizing that it was hypocritical and contradictory.*

Kawai: Well, I think it comes down to the type of hypocrisy. I mean, even America is hypocritical – extremely hypocritical.

Murakami: *Definitely.*

Kawai: They say they are trying to protect Kuwait, but when you get right down to it, it was wrong to create Kuwait in the first place.

Murakami: *Yes, you're right.*

Kawai: In other words, we use a very ambiguous form of hypocrisy to deal with countries like this that are engaged in clearly hypocritical acts. In the end, which way of thinking is more effective? I would say that the ambiguous approach is ultimately more productive.

This is the sort of thing I've been thinking about a lot lately – instead of fearing contradiction or taking issue with inconsistency, trying to place the emphasis on balance.

Murakami: *That's exactly what I'm trying to do in my novels and stories at the moment. As I see it, balance is an extremely important element in a novel. There's no real need for consistency, and integrity and order aren't major concerns either.*

Kawai: That viewpoint also comes through in *The Wind-Up Bird Chronicle*. Deliberately using the word 'chronicle' in the title makes it even more interesting. When we hear the word 'chronicle,' we usually imagine something arranged in a clear chronological order. But that's not the way it is in *The Wind-Up Bird Chronicle*.

Murakami: *That's right.*

9. Self-Healing and Novels

Murakami: *As for why I started writing novels, I don't really know myself, but one day, out of the blue, I felt the need to write. Thinking back on it now, it seems as if that was the first step in a kind of self-healing process.*

I spent my 20s working away madly without giving a thought to anything else, and somehow I managed to survive. Then, at the age of 29, I found myself at a kind of landing in the staircase. It wasn't exactly sandplay, but for some reason that I can't completely explain, I decided I wanted to present unexplainable things in the form of a novel. It really happened all of a sudden.

Up until that point, I had never thought about trying to write a novel; I had just worked. Then one day I thought, "That's it! I'll write a novel," so I went to buy a fountain pen and some manuscript paper, and after I finished working, I would diligently write for an hour or two in the kitchen. That made me feel very happy. I found it very difficult to convey things that I couldn't really explain in the form of a novel, and I had to revise my work over and over again. But when I was finished, I felt as if a huge burden had been lifted from my shoulders. This led me to aphorisms and detachment – things that were completely unlike anything I had ever seen in a Japanese novel.

It was impossible for me to say what I wanted to say in the style of conventional Japanese novels. I think that's why it took me so long to write.

Murakami: *Self-healing and Novels*

As I mentioned in the conversation, writing novels is in large part an act of self-healing. Some people might set out to convey a particular message through a novel, but for me at least, this isn't the case. Instead, I write novels to discover the messages within me. In the process of writing a story, these messages suddenly appear out of the darkness – though in many cases, they are written in an indecipherable code.

I think writing novels is similar to playing a role-playing video game. By that I mean that you never know what's going to appear on the screen next, you maintain a neutral focus, your fingers are lightly positioned on the buttons, and you have to deal swiftly with unforeseen circumstances that suddenly arise. And in many cases, the way that you respond to a situation has novelistic significance.

But what's decisively different from role-playing games at the game center is that in writing, the program that you are using is one that you yourself made. As you create the program, you are simultaneously acting as a player. And as you play the game, your memory of programming is completely erased. Your left hand doesn't know what the right hand's doing, and vice versa. For me, this is the ultimate game and also a form of self-healing. Actually doing it, though, is very difficult.

But I knew that that still wasn't enough for me to make it as a novelist. So I gradually started converting the aphorisms and detachment into stories. My first book was a full-length novel called A Wild Sheep Chase. Since then, my books have become longer and longer. Unless I make them long, the story doesn't really seem complete.

Another reason for their length is that the story has to be spontaneous. To me, it would be meaningless to systematically plot out every detail. So I spontaneously create a succession of things, and then finally I come to the ending. If there wasn't an ending, it wouldn't be a novel.

When I start writing, I don't have a rough sketch of the story or anything like that. I just immerse myself in the act of writing and then, as they say, the ending kind of comes naturally. And since I'm supposed to be a professional writer, there's always an ending. That provides a certain amount of catharsis.

Writing stories in this way has made my books longer and longer. I kept on going like this until Hard-Boiled Wonderland and the End of the World.

Murakami: *There's Always an Ending*

Simply put, what I meant by, "since I'm a professional writer, there's always an ending," is that without an ending, I wouldn't be able to support myself as a novelist. This also includes an aspect of believing in yourself. The rest is experience. Even so, I still have times when I wonder if something is really okay or not, but I continue writing as I persuade myself that it is.

Then to move up to the next level, I decided I needed to teach myself how to write more realistically, so I wrote Norwegian Wood. *That was the first full-length novel I wrote after leaving Japan.*

The Wind-Up Bird Chronicle *was really a big turning point for me. After I started writing stories, I was simply pleased that the story was a story. Then I think I moved on to the next step.*

The Wind-Up Bird Chronicle *is the third step. First, there were aphorisms and detachment, then there was the storytelling phase, but eventually, I realized there was still something missing. It was at that point that commitment came into play, though this is something I still haven't completely processed.*

I think of commitment as a link between people, but not the old, "I-know-exactly-where-you're-coming-from, let's-join-hands"-kind of thing. I am very drawn to the kind of commitment that involves digging a deeper and deeper well, and forming links by surmounting barriers that seem insurmountable.

But I'm not entirely sure what I can offer in terms of the real world or actual life. This is something I've been considering since I came back to Japan. I've resolved this problem in my novels, but my novels have moved on ahead and I'm still lagging behind. One thing for certain is that the world is in the process of changing and that change is necessary.

That's why I'm very interesting in each turning point, whether it be the earthquake, Aum, or whatever. Though these incidents are deeply tragic in themselves, they give us an opportunity to, as it were, "turn misfortune into fortune," and I have a hunch that they're going to lead to something new.

Also, when I watch TV, I have a strong impression that they're not reporting on anything remotely important and no one is giving any thought to what they're doing.

Kawai: That's certainly true. News coverage conforms to general interest, so it's safe to say that they're not dealing with the fundamental questions when they discuss Aum.

In regard to commitment, Aum appealed to young people who felt the need to commit themselves to something by saying things like, "Commit yourself to this!" and "We have the answer!"

Murakami: *The thing is, the image or the narrative that the group presented was extremely childish.*

Kawai: Yes, it was very childish. That's because they were never trained to use their imagination. The people who joined Aum were taught to follow

---

Murakami: *The Childishness of the Aum Story*

Despite what I said here, I can't help but react strongly to the childish power of the incident. Roughly speaking, it has the same kind of effect on people that 'youth,' 'pure love,' and 'justice' once did. And this is why it was so effective. With this in mind, I don't think it's possible to simply dismiss the case as childish and meaningless.

In a way, stories have become excessively specialized and complicated (be it a novel, a personal story, or a social

ook. Imagination is nowhere to be found in
nd of education. People with rich imagina-
tions are hopeless at textbook learning.

---

*narrative) in our advanced capitalist society. They are also
too sophisticated. Perhaps people actually desire something
more childish. I think it's necessary for us to reexamine the
current state of the narrative. Unless we do, the same sort of
incident is likely to occur again.*

10. Making Stories, Living Stories

Murakami: *I talked earlier about how I had moved from detachment to storytelling and how I have moved away from that now too. Of course, I am continuing to explore things that are related to storytelling, but I'm no longer interested in straight storytelling. What does this mean?*

Kawai: A story can never exist without a foundation of images. And when you have deeply personal images that you want to share with other people, the only way to do it is with a story.

It sounds to me as if, during the phase that you refer to as storytelling, you focused a little bit too much on making the story interesting, and the link to your personal images became diluted. The joy of storytelling in itself doesn't have any staying power. That makes it necessary to renew the link to the imagination – or what you referred to as 'well-digging.' Then the main concern becomes committing yourself to this link to the imagination. If the images and story aren't alive, they lose their power.

Murakami: *In the past, a lot of my novels took the form of legends like the Holy Grail – a search for something that vanishes at the end. But in* The Wind-Up Bird Chronicle, *'recovery' became a very important issue. I think this also marked a transition for me as a person.*

Kawai: It seems as if the story has been completed with the third volume of *The Wind-Up Bird Chronicle.* I've heard some younger people say that they felt relieved when that volume came out – a lot of people have said that that saved them.

Murakami: *The thing is – and I realize this is going to sound extremely arrogant –, it takes a little longer to really understand* The Wind-Up Bird Chronicle.

There are novels that you can digest immediately and there are novels that take more time. For example, I would say that Hard-Boiled Wonderland and the End of the World *is another one that takes quite a while to process. On the other hand, you can quickly digest* A Wild Sheep Chase, *and* Norwegian Wood *is almost immediate. The* Wind-Up Bird Chronicle *is the type of novel that takes more time.*

I feel like the novel has already moved on ahead and now I'm chasing after the images in it.

Kawai: In other words, you still need to actualize them.

Murakami: *Yes, but that's an extremely difficult thing to do.*

Kawai: Right, especially here in Japan.

Kawai: On the Story of Aum

I am in complete agreement with Murakami's comment that stories may have become overly specialized, complicated, and sophisticated. As for his suggestion that people might fundamentally desire stories that are more 'childish,' I would use the word 'simple' instead.

I think that contemporary people are guilty of acclaiming stories based on their complexity, specialization (read: unintelligibility), and sophistication. But I wouldn't argue that the simpler something is, the better it is. The question is, what kind of criteria are used to assess a simple story. To rephrase this, as Murakami suggests, it would be overly hasty to decide that something is meaningless just because it's childish.

I think the problem with the Aum story is that it is a story in which the participants attempted to incorporate a completely alien substance – contemporary technology – into a simple narrative.

In order to reconsider the current state of the narrative, I have dealt with folk tales and children's literature in the past. Though these are extremely childish stories from an adult's perspective, I set out to convey the fact that they actually contain profound meanings. This has led some people to conclude that my books are also childish, so I am grateful to have a chance to occasionally express my opinions about 'adult books' by meeting people like Murakami.

11. Marriage and 'Well-digging'

Murakami: *I'm planning to write a nonfiction book and right now I'm doing some research for it. I decided to take a break from novels and concentrate on this project this year. I wanted to set a specific theme, research it extensively, talk to as many people as I could, and compile everything into a 'non-novel.' Doing this seemed important for me in many different ways. I had the feeling that listening to lots of people's stories would somehow be a healing experience. I guess I wanted to approach other people's*

Murakami: *On Nonfiction*

It's difficult to explain, but my decision to write nonfiction is based not only on what I say here. There are also a few other reasons. The biggest one is that I wanted to understand the significance of a given event. The only way to do this was to write something, and to write something, it was necessary to investigate the facts. And if I was really going to do that, I wanted to do it in a thorough way.

Another reason was that I wanted to know more about the relationships between Japanese people. To do that, I wanted to meet as many people as I could, and listen to what they had *stories head on... Do you think that's going to be difficult?*

Kawai: That's exactly what we do as therapists. In the end, being healed and healing is a form of mutual assistance. It really all depends on the person you're dealing with. The deeper your relationship becomes with the person, the more dangerous it can become.

Murakami: *Are there cases when the person's problems are transferred to the therapist?*

Kawai: Yes, there are.

Murakami: *Do you ever have times when you feel depressed?*

Kawai: Sure, I often get depressed. I feel depressed, but at the same time, I try to engage people in idle chat.

---

to say about the theme. Saying I was trying to 'heal myself' might be too simplistic. To put it more precisely, I think I wanted to blend two elements, one based on a story that I told, and the other based on the stories that other people told.

I can't judge whether The Wind-Up Bird Chronicle *is a good book or not. But writing it was an extremely important thing for me personally. I think it probably took me about three years to recover from the experience. That isn't why I turned to nonfiction, but I had a strong desire to reexamine truth and reality. I was also hoping that this might be useful for other people. To some degree, I took this approach as a way of committing to society.*

Murakami: *You mean you only accept certain parts of the person's extremely serious problem?*

Kawai: It's much more than partial acceptance. That's why my body sometimes feels odd or the person's condition is transferred to me. For example, if I'm dealing with someone who has a habit of going to the bathroom frequently, I might start doing the same, or I might start using certain expressions that the person uses. That sort of thing is quite common.

When that happens, you have to be able to take an objective view of yourself. If you completely accept the other person and enter the same state, you can't treat them. We are always in very close proximity to this danger zone, so it's not unusual to feel exhausted and as if you yourself might die.

Recently, because I deal with people on a deeper level than I ever have in the past, when someone in very poor condition visits me, I also start feeling tired. It's a much more straightforward relationship than it used to be.

Murakami: *There was something else I wanted to ask you. Do married couples have mutually therapeutic relationships?*

Kawai: Yes, I think that's a very strong part of marriage. That's why the pain they feel is also so acute. If one partner wants to understand the other one, they have to do more than talk to them in a rational way, they have to 'dig a well.'

Murakami: *I've been married for over 25 years, and I'm a strong believer in that. But because this subject is so vivid and so close to me, I haven't been able to write about it.*

For the most part, the protagonists in my novels are alone. There aren't any parents in my books. There aren't any kids either. And wives have only made rare appearances. It's mostly friends and prostitutes and people like that. But finally in The Wind-Up Bird Chronicle, *I was able to write about a married couple.*

Kawai: I think it's a really great book in terms of its depiction of marriage.

At the moment, I'm working on a paper about marriage. The idea that two people who love each other get married and live happily ever after is totally absurd. Believing this when you get married causes you to feel depressed later. I've come to the conclusion that people get married and live together as a couple to suffer and dig wells. Well-digging is a very difficult thing, and there's no real reason for people to endure it.

Murakami: *That's a helpful piece of advice.*

Kawai: If it's gotten to the point where you're always moaning about how unhappy you are, and bothering the people around you, then divorce is certainly one option.

Murakami: *Some people get married again and again – three or four times.*

Kawai: Those are generally people who are not willing to dig a well. Digging a well is tiring, so instead of digging they start searching all over for someone new, but they end up with the same kind of person again.

Murakami: *There are also people who get divorced, and even if they get married to someone else for a while, they eventually marry the first person again.*

Murakami: *Getting Married to Suffer*

I found Kawai's definition of marriage as a form of suffering very refreshing and interesting. But hearing this idea expressed in such a clear way can't help but make you feel perplexed.

After many years of marriage, I had the sense that married life was a way of making up for each other's failings. But recently (despite having been married for 25 years), I started to think that things are actually a bit different. Isn't marriage actually an ongoing process of exposing each other's failings (whether in a loud or quiet way)?

Ultimately, the only one who can make up for your failings is you yourself. It isn't something that anyone else can help you with. And in attempting to do this, it is necessary to clearly recognize where and how big your failings are. In the final analysis, I started to think that married life might be nothing more than a cold act of mutual surveillance. Needless to say, this is only my personal opinion. Whatever the case, it's a frightening thing to consider.

Kawai: Right, they repeat the same thing over and over.

In the old days, a couple would just cooperate with each other in various ways, and when they were through, they would die – that in itself was enough. But now people want to do more than simply cooperate; they want to understand each other. If you really want to understand your partner, then you've got to dig a well.

Murakami: *When I was writing* The Wind-Up Bird Chronicle, *I suddenly remembered the couple in Soseki Natsume's novel,* The Gate. *My couple was completely different from Natsume's couple, but I kept an image of them in a corner of my mind. The husband in Natsume's story eventually becomes a Buddhist priest.*

Kawai: He becomes a priest, but later he goes back to his wife, doesn't he? As Natsume shows, you can't really understand marriage through the priesthood, you have to go back and dig a well.

Kawai: Getting Married to Suffer
    This remark was meant to emphasize a particular facet of marriage. I would also like to point out that later in the conversation, I talked about how interesting marriage is. Anything that's really interesting contains a certain amount of pain.
    I feel exactly the same about marriage being a "frightening thing to consider."

In that sense, *The Wind-Up Bird Chronicle* is really a story of strong commitment.

Murakami: *That was an extremely important subject for me. The main character is forced to make a commitment by various characters in the book. The little girl, Mei Kasahara, for example, forces him to make a commitment and then…*

Kawai: And another character, Creta Kano, invites him to go to Crete.

Murakami: *Right, and there's also Lieutenant Mamiya, who entrusts his life to him. He is forced to commit in a variety of different ways. Only his wife Kumiko escapes – she leaves him. But what he really wants to commit to is her.*

Kawai: Depending on the way you look at it, maybe all of the people he committed to until that point were a pathway for him to commit to Kumiko.

Murakami: *At the beginning of the story, he still isn't qualified to commit himself to Kumiko. When he goes down into the well, I see that as a kind of trial (like the one in* The Magic Flute *) – a way for him to become qualified. But this didn't occur to me until I was done with the book.*

12. Married Couples and Other People

Kawai: Sometimes, even in real life, there are cases when a wife or husband suddenly turns invisible.

Murakami: *Turns invisible…?*

Kawai: You made a valiant effort to understand the other person, but then you realized that it was just impossible. You thought that you were living together up until that point and that you understood your partner, but all of a sudden you can't understand them anymore.

Murakami: *Right.*

Kawai: When you reach that point, it's extremely difficult to embark on a new effort to understand them, and in many cases, you start to blame your partner, saying things like, "I don't get that guy" or "Men are worthless."

Murakami: *The thing that really strikes me about American couples is that when they're together, they* *seem to be really close and clingy. Like when they go out somewhere together, they always hold hands. But despite that, when they break up, they break up very suddenly. There are very few cases like that in Japan. Here, even though a couple doesn't like each other, they stay together because of the kids or something.*

Kawai: Another thing about Americans is that they are conscious of the fact that their relationships are somehow not real.

Murakami: *How do you mean?*

Kawai: That's why it's necessary for them to constantly and consciously cling to each other. Unless they constantly reaffirm their love for each other on a conscious level, they become unbearably anxious. Then when it becomes possible to verify their feelings, they suddenly break up.

From a positive perspective, Japanese people don't make an effort to reaffirm their relationship. It's the same sort of devious philosophy that we talked about earlier; they have a vague feeling that they're in harmony with each other. That approach to married life seems more interesting to me.

Murakami: *Because it includes all kinds of different aspects?*

Kawai: Yes. In the West, romantic love is inevitably the model. But romantic love is not enduring. If you want to maintain a romantic relationship in the long term, you have to have a sexual relationship. But I don't think it's possible to sustain romantic love while having a sexual relationship. In order for a couple to continue a relationship, they have to enter another dimension.

Murakami: *A sexual relationship has a kind of healing effect. But at a certain point it has to change into another form of healing... Maybe that's when 'well-digging' becomes necessary.*

Kawai: I think so. A sexual relationship is very important while you're young, and it does have a healing effect, but there has to be more than that.

Murakami: *Do you think that people who can't make the transition to well-digging at that point start looking for another kind of sexual healing?*

Kawai: Romantic Love and Japan

In Japan, marriage was originally most important as a social and collective institution. Love was even deemed bad, as it threatened to upset the established order. Romantic love emerged solely from an emphasis on the individual.

When the original goal of shaping the individual character, in part rooted in religion, became linked to secular marriage, it led to a variety of difficulties of the sort that can also be seen in America.

Japanese people try to imitate Westerners, but it is extremely difficult for us to grasp the essence of romantic love. However, since our efforts are rather slipshod, the dangers they bring are also not as great, and this helps keep the peace between married couples.

Kawai: Certainly. They start looking around and begin another sexual relationship. In Japan, we call this kind of thing an "in-home divorce." In their hearts, the couple is divorced, but for the time being they're still living in the same house.

Or another thing that happens in Japan is that people completely stop trying to expand their world through the opposite sex. For example, they might become a scholar and embark on some elaborate research project. They channel their sexual desire in a different direction. If you channel your desire toward a woman, it can be very difficult because she's alive, so you might channel your feelings into something like researching old documents instead. That allows you to develop a strong passion – you become interested in the places in the documents that were eaten by insects and trying to decipher certain words in them – and it's much less dangerous.

Murakami: *Or you could also put all your energy into your job.*

Kawai: Exactly. There are lots of people who channel their sexual desires into something other than a living person.

Murakami: *But you can't make a sweeping statement and say that one is better than the other.*

Kawai: No, you can't. In the end, it just depends on how you choose to live your life. Maybe there aren't really that many people who place a strong emphasis on marriage. Personally, I think marriage is extraordinarily interesting. What could be more interesting than that?

I also think that in Japan marriage provides a lot of people with a way of understanding religion.

Murakami: *To me, marriage seems like a kind of struggle.*

Kawai: Really? Ultimately, there's no way of finding a perfect answer, and you begin to realize that there's some kind of being or spirit that lies beyond your control. That's why I think marriage can be a gateway to understanding religion. Of course, there's no particular reason why you have to do that either.

Murakami: *As long as you enjoy researching old documents, that's enough.*

Kawai: The only thing is, you have to be careful. If a man enjoys looking at old documents, but his wife starts putting a lot of effort into their marriage, it can lead to tragic consequences. If the wife doesn't care about the marriage either, and puts all of her energy into her children or making pickles or something, the situation is probably more or less stable.

I think there are various kinds of relationships, and you can't really say one is better than another. But I would hope that each person is at least aware of what they're doing – because we can sometimes become a neighborhood nuisance.

Murakami: *Neighborhood nuisance?*

Kawai: Let's say, the husband is putting a lot of work into old documents, but his wife is deeply troubled about their relationship. As long as the man is into his documents and his wife enjoys taking care of the kids, everything is fine.

But if the wife wants a closer marital relationship, the husband's actions can cause the wife a great deal of pain. That's why I say that everyone should always consider whether their actions are harming other people. Perhaps this is a Western viewpoint, but ultimately it's a question of personal responsibility.

The Second Night: Dredging Up the

Unconscious – Body and Mind

13. Stories and the Body

Murakami: *Until I started writing novels, I wasn't particularly interested in my body. But after I started writing, I became deeply interested in my own physical and physiological state, and I began exercising. In the process, my body changed – my pulse, my muscles, my physique. At the same time, I became very aware that my novels and writing style were also undergoing a rapid change. Do physical and mental changes act in concert with each other?*

Kawai: Yes, it seems obvious that they do. For example, a long time ago writers saw their work as something that was only related to words and the mind, so the body was of no concern to them and they tended to ignore or disdain it. Excessive drinking was one expression of this disdain. The writing that emerged as a result is completely different from writing like yours that is a product of physical training.

In that sense, old Japanese writers probably didn't give much thought to incorporating an element of physicality into their writing and work.

Murakami: *Maybe that also had to do with the times they lived in.*

Kawai: A long time ago there seems to have been a tendency to see the body and mind as separate entities. Modern thinking certainly has an aspect of this. Recently, people have begun to understand that things aren't quite that simple.

Though not quite Cartesian, the modern era was founded on the notion of a division between mind and body. This extremely simplistic view held that because the mind was important, the body wasn't.

Murakami: *The idea that there is a clear divide between the two has become very rare among young people today.*

Murakami: *On the Younger Generation's View of the Body*

One thing for certain is that over the years there has been a growing tendency to link physical values with mental values. In other words, due to an overemphasis on the mind, there has been a shift toward the notion that, "anything is okay if it feels good." I see this as an extension of 1960s counterculture and drug experiences. There's nothing wrong with it per se – it's just another state of mind.

But having reached a certain age, things don't seem quite as simple as that to me. Just flopping down on the lawn isn't going to make an apple fall off the tree. If you want things to keep feeling good, it's necessary to put in a certain amount of

Kawai: Yes, I think there's been a definite change. That also explains why a variety of difficult issues related to sex have emerged. In the end, sex is something that lies between the mind and the body.

Murakami: *When I set out to write a story, physical strength is essential. Without concentration or endurance, I wouldn't be able to draw out the story.*

In my case, my stories have become longer and longer. In other words, my books have gotten thicker. If I hadn't built up my endurance and concentration, I don't think it would have been physically possible to do this.

Conversely, I have the vague feeling that reviving that kind of huge narrative wouldn't be possible unless it was connected to reviving some kind of physicality.

One of my favorite American writers is John Irving. I see him as the person who resurrected the narrative in contemporary America. He is very fond of physical activity and he's still active as a wrestling coach. I was hoping to do an interview with Irving when I went to meet him, but he said, "I don't have

---

effort. It seems to me that believing that everything is going to be simple and easy will eventually lead to things like drugs and prostitution. I don't want to sound tedious, but I believe there is a need for some sort of ethical stance to go with the new era. This is likely to be a more flexible philosophy with physicality as a keynote, but I think the big question has to do with the power to definitively eliminate delusional violence (such as Aum's).

much time, so why don't you come running with me in Central Park?" So I interviewed him as we ran and I think that really had a big impact on my view of the writer's life.

Another thing is that unless you're strong, you could never do something like "pass through walls."* It's necessary to have fighting spirit – without that, you're destined to lose. In this sense, the first thing you need is strength.

It's like going down to the bottom of a well and entering a kind of netherworld. This type of purification – physical purification – is very important.

Kawai: Whether you're going down into a well or passing through walls, the image would be very different without physical strength. Even if you could pass through a wall, it wouldn't have any punch.

If the whole thing were a mental construct, it wouldn't be worth a second thought. It wouldn't work at all. I often refer to this type of thing as a 'made-up story.' A made-up story is something without the body, something that was created purely with the mind. This type of thing doesn't really hold the reader's attention.

It's difficult for Japanese people to understand the difference, and there are people who create what they call 'fantasies' but which are really just

---

*Editors note: "Passing through walls" is a kind of supernatural phenomenon that occurs on a subconscious level (see the second volume of *The Wind-Up Bird Chronicle*).

made-up stories. The kind of stories you're talking about rely on the body.

Murakami: *In sandplay, is there a difference between things that are made-up and things with a physical aspect?*

Kawai: In sandplay therapy, you can make whatever you want, so it's okay to create something that simply looks nice without making any special commitment. All you have to do is put a few things down and say, "Voilà!" But that approach isn't very interesting to the person doing it or to the person watching it.

For instance, in one course I did on sandplay therapy, someone created a mandala made up of all kinds of beautiful flowers. But when we look at something like that as therapists, we are completely

---

Kawai: On "Giving It Your All"

It's difficult for most people to comprehend the idea that having an extraordinary amount of energy makes it possible to "pass through walls."

But when you have that much energy, you can really pull that kind of thing off. Instead of thinking about it, you use so much concentration and strength that it is actually possible to go down into the well and pass through the walls. But unless an image of passing through the wall emerges of its own accord, it would never work.

It's something that supersedes thought. Doing something that exceeds your abilities can also sometimes lead to physical illness because you're employing a considerable amount of strength.

unimpressed. When I asked the man why he made it, he said, "Sandplay therapy is all about making mandalas, right?" Someone had apparently told him that you had to make a mandala, so that's what he did. It wasn't something that actually came from inside of him.

Murakami: *But there are people who make things that come from inside of themselves, right?*

Kawai: Yes, everyone is deeply moved when something like that happens. It's really amazing.

Murakami: *What makes it so different?*

Kawai: You can somehow feel the amount of energy the person has invested in their work.

Murakami: *But aren't the people who make these things suffering from some kind of illness or problem?*

Kawai: No, in this case it was just a training course.

Murakami: *Oh, you mean they were just regular people not patients?*

Kawai: Yes, it's altogether different with sick people. The things they make are deeply moving.

Murakami: *Each in its own particular way?*

Kawai: Yes, each person has something that they really have to express. But if you ask someone suffering from an illness to do sandplay and they feel frightened, it won't work.

Murakami: *Do some of them create made-up stories?*

Kawai: They can't do that because they're suffering from some sort of emotional disorder.

Murakami: *They can't?*

Kawai: No, it's impossible. They can't escape from their situation. The only thing they can do is stop coming or stop doing sandplay.

Murakami: *So when they make things, does some kind of story start to emerge?*

Kawai: If you look at photographs documenting the changes in their sandplay, even an amateur has a pretty good sense of what's going on.

On the other hand, when a person without any particular problems does sandplay, it is remarkably uninteresting. In other words, so-called normal or healthy people have a special talent for making boring or non-deviant things.

Murakami: *In other words, waking up in the morning, going to work, doing your job, and coming home is a kind of talent.*

Kawai: Yes, that's a talent.

Murakami: *But among the things that sick people make there must be varying levels of quality – very interesting, so-so, interesting, and so on.*

Kawai: Yes, to a certain extent. There are different levels in terms of depth, and some of the things people make are truly amazing.

On the other hand, when so-called healthy people really commit themselves to sandplay, the results can be amazing. In order for that to happen, though, the conditions must be very good.

Murakami: *Is there a proportional relationship between the severity of the person's illness and the impact of their work?*

Kawai: No, it doesn't really work like that. It's a difficult thing. If the illness is too severe, it's impossible to express the whole thing. In that case, the person can only express part of it, and the feeling that they want to escape from the situation takes precedence. So the severity of the illness and the impact of the work don't really correspond to each other.

Kawai: Amazing Sandplay

Here, I was using the word "amazing" to suggest the strong impact that a work can have on a viewer, a surprising expression, a series of unexpected developments, and an aesthetically impressive work.

Murakami: *When people become sick, do we all have the potential ability to make stories?*

Kawai: It's difficult to say. In a sense, every human being is sick, and even though someone might be ill, unless they have the strength to express the illness, it will never take a concrete form. People with illnesses are simply overwhelmed by a feeling of fatigue or dread, so in some cases it takes a long time for a story to emerge.

Murakami: *If all people are in a sense sick, can we also assume that artists and creators are sick?*

Kawai: Of course.

Murakami: *And on top of this, we have to stay healthy.*

Kawai: Yes, you must have the strength to express something in a given form. Artists are people who also have the ability to take on the illnesses of their age and culture.

While they suffer from their own personal illnesses, they also have the ability to overcome them. This allows them to take on the illnesses of their age and culture, and imbues their artistic expressions with a sense of universality.

14. The Relationship between a Work and Its Author

Murakami: *Personally, I think I am someone who is somewhat ill. Or rather than ill, it might be better to say that there's something missing. Since all human beings are in some sense missing something from the time they're born, each of us tries different things to make up for our failings. In my case, I was over 30 when I started to write, and I think this was my way of trying to make up for my failings.*

But no matter how much you try to make up for them, you can never complete the process. At first you might be able to do it with something simple, but gradually it takes more and more to compensate for them. Do you think that the creative act is somehow rooted in this kind of feeling?

Kawai: I think so. It is also necessary for these attempts or expressions to in some way communicate something to other people. This requires a great deal of technique and ingenuity. And in order to endure, you also have to closely examine the techniques and patterns that you have acquired and constantly try to supersede them.

Murakami: *The thing that amazes me is that people like Mozart or Schubert were only active for a very short period of time. They emerged in a very natural way and then all of a sudden they were gone. Of course, part of it probably had to do with the fact that their bodies just couldn't keep up.*

On the other hand, there were also people like Beethoven and Mahler, who developed in a cumulative and dialectic way.

Kawai: It just depends on the person – you can't really do anything about it. Mozart certainly seems to have been a victim of his own creativity.

Murakami: *I think I'm more of a cumulative, dialectic type.*

Murakami: *Making Up for Our Failings*

I think I should explain the phrase "making up for my failures." First of all, let me stress that these failings (or illnesses) are in no way negative aspects of our lives. It's natural to have some failings. But when you're earnestly attempting to express something, it isn't so easy to accept that your failings are natural or fine. So we try to make up for them somehow. When there is a certain degree of objectivity involved in this act, it can result in art. That's what I was trying to get at.

Kawai: *The Wind-Up Bird Chronicle* conveys that impression very strongly. That probably means that you'll be able to create a lot more work in the future.

Murakami: *What gave you that impression?*

Kawai: First of all, the book has a clear structure. Old Japanese I-novels didn't have any structure.

With *The Wind-Up Bird Chronicle*, there are various structural issues, like whether it would be better to end the book after the second volume or the third one. The structure is amazing because you decided to keep going until the third volume. Besides that, we are left with a lot of mysteries. So it seems to me that, at this rate, you'll be able to keep going for some time.

Murakami: *The thing about* The Wind-Up Bird Chronicle *is that even I don't have a clue what it all means. It's been the same with every book I've ever written – I don't understand them.*

Kawai: Regarding the I-Novel

In Japan, the distinction between the self and others is not as clear as it is in the West. Even though you might use the word 'I' in Japanese, it is really identical to the 'world.' I-novels, which make ingenious use of this ambiguity, focus on something completely different from what Western people refer to as 'I myself.' The reason these books succeeded was because they set out to equate various personal matters with the world at large. However, it is very difficult to translate this appeal to another culture.

Although I used a fairly similar approach in Hard-Boiled Wonderland and the End of the World, I had a much better grasp of what was going on in that book.

But this time I don't have any idea what's what. For example, even as the writer, I don't know why a certain thing happened or what kind of meaning it might have. That was a big thing for me, and for that reason alone, I had to exert a great deal of energy.

Kawai: Works of art always have this aspect. If they didn't, they wouldn't be interesting. If the author already understood everything, it wouldn't be art. Mystery novels are based on a particular device, but when it comes to a work of art, it's natural for the author to have lots of things they don't understand.

They somehow know how things should go. If you started out by thinking about the meaning of certain things, it would never work.

Murakami: *Of course, I can read and consider the text in the same way that other people and critics read it. The most troubling thing, though, is that when I express an opinion about the text as a reader, it is considered to be my opinion as the writer.*

Kawai: There are some people who believe that the author's comments are the most accurate. That's completely ludicrous.

Murakami: *When I said this to university students in America, they got angry. For example, in my seminars we would read some of my short stories, and then they would say, "Mr. Murakami, what do you think?" I would tell them what I thought and then I'd say, "But this is just one opinion – the same as yours." Then they'd say, "But you wrote it, didn't you?"*

Is that a common tendency in America?

Kawai: Americans put great stock in the Western-style ego, so there is a strong reliance on one's own intentions and ideas. They tend to believe that what the writer says about his writing is correct.

In Europe, things are a bit different. Europe has a longer history and Europeans have experienced all kinds of odd things.

In America, however, there is a strong tendency to believe that the ego equals the person. This is connected to ideas like, "I started this company myself. It's all down to my hard work, and I did it exactly like I wanted to do. Anything wrong with that? If that guy can't do the same, it's his own fault." I imagine that Americans approach works of art in the same way. There has to be something that transcends the person who made them or they're not interesting.

15. Stories as a Link between People

Murakami: *There was a time when stories lost their power, but they seem to be making a comeback now. A long time ago, stories were completely unrelated to physicality and simply existed.*

Kawai: In those days, stories tended to include both physical and mental aspects without expressing any particularly difficult ideas. There wasn't any need to talk about things like the difference between stories and novels, because that was all there was.

But as time went on, the subject of the story, which had at one point been negated, reemerged, and it became necessary to be conscious of many narrative aspects, including the logic of physicality that we're now discussing.

A long time ago, the various investigations that are currently underway in what is called 'post-modernism' would have met with causal indifference. That's why I like old tales and stories so much.

This is my own hypothesis, but I believe that stories have the power to create all kinds of different connections – they are a very powerful way to link things like the body and mind, the inner world and the outer world, and men and women. More than that, contemporary people are aware enough to separate these things and put them back together again, whereas a long time ago, stories weren't divided in the way they are now.

Later, stories became unpopular because they were considered to be unreal. But in ancient times, there wasn't a clear division between stories and reality.

In the West, or more precisely, the Christian world, the Bible was written to create a link between people and God. And because it was considered to be an absolutely orthodox bible or book, nothing else was permitted. Creating another story was seen as an act of sacrilege. That's probably why it took so long for stories to emerge in the West. Then at last, *The Decameron*, a story in which human beings were slightly more powerful in regard to God, appeared.

Murakami: *That was in the Renaissance, right?*

Kawai: Yes. Another book had finally appeared. On the other hand, the reason it did was that it was anti-Christian. It was necessary to create a story that to some extent opposed God. As I see it, that's how those stories came to be.

In Japan, though, we didn't have that kind of powerful god, so a succession of stories emerged spontaneously.

Murakami: *But I have the sense that Murasaki Shikibu was very conscious of what she was doing. The way she wrote* The Tale of Genji *and its narrative structure are extremely complex. I can't imagine that a story like that could have appeared out of thin air...*

Kawai: You're probably right. Every story has to be created, so there must also be an individual there to create it. In that sense, women during that period [the 11th century] lived in an environment that allowed them to function as individuals.

In other words, men were deeply involved in an organized system. And women of a higher social standing were, too, but the women who played supporting roles, including Murasaki Shikubu, were very free. That explains why most of the stories from that period were written by women. It's hard to imagine men writing them.

Murakami: *In effect, the women occupied a place outside of the social system.*

Kawai: Yes, they were slightly removed and they had time. They also had money – so in effect they had everything they needed. And no matter how much they tried, they could never improve their social status. Those were the conditions they found themselves in and because they were also very intelligent, they were able to pour all of their energy into writing stories.

Kawai: Women as Individuals

At that time, women weren't part of the Japanese system. They also had a certain amount of time and money, and they weren't particularly interested in achieving success or accumulating wealth. These conditions are just as applicable to present-day Japanese women who are involved in creative work. More women than men exhibit a free-wheeling, vigorous style of creativity. In contemporary Japan, it is unusual to find a male 'samurai'; most of them are women.

16. Beyond Cause and Effect

Murakami: *Are the supernatural elements in* The Tale of Genji *actually part of reality?*

Kawai: Supernatural elements?

Murakami: *What I mean is…*

Kawai: Oh yes, I think they're completely real.

Murakami: *Rather than being a narrative device, they're part of reality?*

Kawai: Yes, I think all of those things really happened; they weren't intended as any kind of device.

Murakami: *But contemporary writers would have no choice but to use them as a kind of narrative device.*

Kawai: That's what makes writing so difficult today.

Murakami: *I have the sense, though, that even if you started out using something like that as a device, at some point it would transcend that function.*

Kawai: I think if you started out using it as a device and it didn't transcend its function, it wouldn't be a work of art. It's necessary to have a certain amount of energy to, as you said earlier, "pass through walls." Without that, there's absolutely no way you can create a work of art. Though at some point, you might consciously decide to use a particular device.

Murakami: *Of course, but we wouldn't actually see these things as part of reality.*

Kawai: Once you entrust the device to the work, it starts to become very interesting.

Murakami: *I have the feeling that [the novelist] Kyoka Izumi was quite aware of this, but it's hard to know for sure.*

Kawai: Japanese Stories

Japanese stories actually tell about 'things' [*monogatari*, the Japanese word for 'story,' literally means 'telling things']. In some cases, even the things do the telling. These 'things' are completely different from Western matter, and extend to many subjects, ranging from human affairs to people's spirits.

This is because they are in some sense real, and a long time ago Japanese people probably saw talking about reality as telling a story. From a contemporary perspective, however, these stories seem to be laden with devices to develop the plot.

Kawai: Yes, that's difficult to judge.

Murakami: *That's why it seems perfectly appropriate that Izumi's work is currently being reassessed. If I remember correctly, his last book has that kind of obscure quality about it.*

Kawai: In a contemporary novel, you can't really write about interesting things that are the result of amazing coincidences. You have to write so that everyone will understand. But there really are lots of interesting coincidences.

Murakami: *That's true.*

Kawai: I have witnessed people being cured, and in the process very interesting coincidences actually do occur. The patient makes it possible for coincidences to happen.

When I come out with something like this, everyone says, "Don't be ridiculous!" But these things really happen, so what can you say? When I simply relate actual events that occur, people say, "That's crazy!" Which means that they have the strange notion that reality should be a certain way.

Contemporary fiction might be based on the premise that interesting coincidences don't often occur, but I would argue that everything is science fiction. Modern novels don't in any way represent reality – they are science-fiction stories. The idea that everything is constrained by science, or that things can only be explained in terms of cause and effect is completely ludicrous. In reality as I know it, there are many coincidences.

Sometimes, half in jest, I'll say to a patient, "You're never going to be cured!" And then I add, "But coincidences do happen, and I'm betting on one happening here." And that's really what happens.

My job is basically to wait for coincidences to happen. Most people don't have the strength to wait for a coincidence to happen, so they search for some kind of certain cure, but they all fail. I don't make any effort to cure them; I just wait for a coincidence to happen.

Murakami: *But it's hard to wait for a coincidence.*

Murakami: *On Fiction*

Recently, people often talk about how the novel has lost its power, but as I mentioned in the conversation, I don't think that's the case at all. The reason that other types of media seem to have transcended the novel is that they provide a volume of information that greatly exceeds that of the novel. And compared to the novel, the speed at which these media transmit information is extraordinarily fast. On top of that, many of these media have greedily engulfed the novel's function and made it their own. That's why it seems increasingly difficult to define what a novel is and how it functions. That much is true.

I would instead argue that the real meaning and merit of the novel lies in the slowness of the response, the small volume of information, and the difficulty (or the awkwardly personal act) of handcrafting it. As long as these things can be maintained, the novel will never lose its power. As time

Kawai: It certainly is – because you're not doing anything. You just wait and when everything goes right and a coincidence occurs, you have to get busy and do the best you can.

Murakami: *After the Aum incident, a lot of critics said things like, "Truth is stranger than fiction." But I don't see it that way. If you just turned that incident into fiction, no one would read it. The narrative devices are extremely shoddy and it's completely unconvincing as a novel. In this case, the idea that truth is stranger than fiction simply doesn't hold water. In fact, truth and fiction should always have a reciprocal relationship to each other. It isn't a question of one being stranger than the other. But a lot of people have been persuaded by this sort of oversimplification.*

---

passes, and this massive tide of direct information ebbs and disappears, people will at last come to understand this.

Surely there is no medium except the novel that allows a poor young man (or woman) with nothing but a heap of delusions to make a heartfelt appeal to the world while also allowing other people to receive this expression – providing, of course, that the writer is lucky.

I think what has actually lost a certain amount of power is literature, an industry founded on the recognition of existing media, and the people who relied on this system. Fiction hasn't lost any of its power. For someone who wants to make some kind of appeal, the possibilities are probably even greater now than they were in the past.

In my view, fiction is always weaker than truth in all kinds of different ways. I don't think there's any such thing as fiction that is stranger than truth.

Kawai: But there are aspects of fiction that are stronger. This is a bit different from what you were saying, but I would suggest that fiction is stronger in the sense that it is created by a single person.

Murakami: *Another strength is the ability of a book like* The Tale of Genji *to evoke a particular era as a landscape. That's something that only fiction can do.*
But in the end, why did Murasaki Shikibu write that book?

Kawai: I'm of the belief that she wrote it as a way of healing herself.

Kawai: On Fiction

I was very pleased to see Murakami list "the slowness of the response, the small volume of information, and the difficulty of handcrafting it," as examples of the novel's merits. Forgive me for constantly focusing on my own concerns, but these are exactly the things I would cite as the merits of psychotherapy. And since I see my job as helping people discover their own story, this proves that I am not far off the mark.

The current tendency to provide the fastest possible response, obtain the greatest amount of information, and mass-produce everything, is the polar opposite of Murakami's writing. Moreover, this tendency is damaging the human soul. In order to help people who are in need of healing, it is important for us to go against the tide. In

Murakami: *In that case, considering that the book is so long, can we assume that she was shouldering a heavy karmic burden?*

Kawai: Yes, I think she was a woman with a great deal of karmic pain.

Murakami: *Is that the sense you get as a contemporary reader?*

Kawai: Yes. She was writing to be healed or to heal herself. Considering what she created, it must have been a tremendous burden.

Murakami: *Does that mean that when you read books you generally approach them from the perspective of a psychotherapist?*

Kawai: No, not at all. In most cases, I approach books purely as a reader. I usually immerse myself in novels and movies, sharing the characters' hopes and fears, and trying to identify with them.

---

that sense, it is a great pleasure for me to discover these similarities between psychotherapy and writing.

Despite this, as I mentioned, individual people's souls are being deeply injured by these trends, and we should carefully consider the irony that these developments have emerged from the West, which is such a vocal advocate of individualism. This way of life, which places such a strong emphasis on the individual, is also the way of life that gave rise to these trends that have deeply injured the individual.

People of my generation often read novels and watched movies when we were adolescents. Then we'd get together and talk about them. Everybody would critique the works, but I could never do that because I identified so closely with the characters. The kind of things I would say were, "Why did he do a stupid thing like that?," or, "If only something had happened right then!" Meanwhile, everyone else was talking about what kind of expression it was or classifying it as a certain -ism.

I didn't know the first thing about that kind of stuff. I felt ashamed of myself, but I have just kept on the same way over all these years, and in the end, it proved to be useful.

Murakami: *You mean, when you're doing sandplay...*

Kawai: The Act of Curing

When you think deeply about 'curing,' it is almost impossible to define. In this case, however, I am using 'curing' in the simple sense of the word to refer to the disappearance of symptoms and the resolution of anxiety.

Murakami: *Novels and Curing*

As I mentioned earlier in the conversation, there are cases in which the writer is cured by writing a novel, but there is also a need to simultaneously heal the reader. Unless you do this, the work is not effective as a novel. Of course, this means curing some part of the reader to a greater or lesser degree – it isn't a magic wand and it isn't effective for everyone everywhere.

But even if it's only partially effective, when it works well, it sends feedback to the writer. And that, in turn,

Kawai: Right. There are pleasant times and there are painful times. Just watching someone do sand-play can sometimes be difficult because I can sense how difficult and painful it is for them.

---

encourages and heals the writer. A lot of writers refer to this as a 'response.' Without this, it's difficult for a writer to continue writing in the long term.

At the same time, however, there is the reverse – rancorous feedback. Positive feedback is inevitably accompanied by negative feedback. You sometimes receive something negative and it can be very painful. But I believe that, without accepting a certain amount of negative feedback or hatred, it is difficult to attain any depth in your writing. I have the feeling that going to that extreme ultimately makes your work genuine.

17. Curing and Living

Murakami: *American psychiatrists often ask their patients to lie down on a couch and take notes as they listen to them talk. Do you do the same kind of thing?*

Kawai: There's a reason for that. In the early years of psychoanalysis, Freud found that emotional transference would sometimes occur in the course of a treatment. For example, a female patient might develop a strong romantic attachment to the analyst. (One doctor named [Eugen] Bleuler, who was associated with Freud, married one of his patients and quit psychiatry.)

Freud believed that this was a transference of infantile emotions to the doctor, and that by analyzing this tendency, you could understand a lot about the patient.

So to establish the fact that transference was occurring, the doctor was supposed to avoid dealing with the patient as a man or woman. By sitting behind them and simply taking notes, the doctor maintained a neutral relationship with the patient. If the patient still professed a fondness for the analyst, this would show that transference was occurring. And this in turn would enable the doctor to analyze where the feeling was coming from.

However, it's also possible for an analyst to develop a fondness for the patient. This is known as countertransference. Countertransference must be avoided at all costs. To do this, it is crucial that the analyst has a deep self-understanding, so they have to undergo a long period of didactic analysis. Then they can analyze patients from a completely neutral position. This was the way people thought in the early days of psychiatry.

In reality, however, patients display a variety of different emotions. By merely listening from behind the patient, the doctor could get paid and begin to analyze the patient by saying something like, "And where did this anger come from?"

But in order to move forward with this type of analysis, the patient had to be strong enough to endure the treatment. Freud clearly stated that patients must have enough strength to analyze themselves objectively along with the analyst. He said people who were too weak to withstand this process should not be subjected to psychoanalysis.

After a while, though, this notion faded, and the idea that we also have a responsibility to help weaker people grew prevalent. The old approach was rejected, and the idea emerged that unless the doctor, as a fellow human being, overcame this type of problem based on their mutual emotions while engaging with the patient, it would be difficult for the patient to make any progress.

Some people continue to use the old method of sitting behind the patient and taking notes, but people like myself sit face-to-face with the patient. If the patient expresses a fondness for me, I talk to them about their feelings, and I don't make any attempt to hide my own feelings.

Murakami: *What do you mean?*

Kawai: What I mean is if, for example, I also like the patient, I tell them that I have come to like them in the same way that they like me, but that at the same time, the fact that two human beings like each other is finally not very important...

Murakami: *Really?*

Kawai: Yes. Well, in one sense it's important, but in another sense it's not. Either way we have to continue with the examination.

We share our feelings with each other like this, but at the same time, I examine the situation from various perspectives as an analyst. We can't allow the situation to develop into anything sticky.

Let's say a female patient comes to see me and says she likes me, and I start liking her too. If it gets to the point where we can't resist this mutual attraction anymore, the only thing to do is suspend the analysis. It's a professional relationship, so you have to say, "I can no longer continue this relationship as a professional, so please go somewhere else." Or you have to quit your job and marry the person. The choices have to be absolutely clear – you can't engage in any deception.

But gradually you grow stronger as a therapist, so when someone likes you a little or even a lot, it doesn't faze you anymore, and you just talk about it with the patient.

To twist things around a little, there are people who say things like, "Doctor, it's all very clear. If I sleep with you, I know I'll be cured. Everything will be fine if we just go to bed together, so let's go." I would then reply, "What you're saying is right. That's exactly how it is, but human beings can't always do the right thing, and unfortunately I can't do the right thing in this case either." I never say anything about the person being wrong. I try to persuade them by talking about the appropriate way to behave as a person. If I responded by blaming them and saying something like, "Are you out of your mind?", the patient would start to hate themselves, or think that they were a very lewd person. They might also make a desperate attempt to explain. So this is a way of expressing the fact that what they said was important.

After all, there's more to it than just being cured. The main thing is living. And that's a very important point.

Murakami: *Although it's not necessary for me as a novelist to deal with people face-to-face, I've been in similar situations. People write me letters saying that their problems have all disappeared after reading my books.*

Kawai: I imagine that's quite a regular occurrence for a writer.

Murakami: *A lot of people say, "Why did you write about me?" or "How do you know me so well?" It runs the gamut from people who are clearly suffering from some sort of mental problem to regular people.*

Kawai: In that sense, the jobs that we do are difficult, but to me this is a necessary element in helping me cure my own illness.

Murakami: *Do you think it's really necessary?*

Kawai: Yes. In many cases, meeting people like that helps me cure my own illness. If I wasn't doing this job, I think I'd become very strange.

18. Individuality and Universality

Kawai: The other day I was talking with Jin Tatsu-mura, the director of the film *Gaia Symphony*. He told me about meeting Jacques Mayol, a diver who plunges 100 meters under the sea.

When Tatsumura asked Mayol why he dived, he said, "I turn into a dolphin." He starts by meditating. He doesn't have an inordinate amount of physical strength or anything like that. He's just a regular guy. But in the process of meditating, he turns into a dolphin. When he feels that the change is complete, he begins diving. And he doesn't use any equipment – he free-dives the entire 100 meters. But being that he's a Westerner, there is also a doctor on standby with an aqualung. He uses a stethoscope and measures various bodily functions.

This revealed that when Mayol is 100 meters under the sea, his pulse rate is 20 beats a minute. Of course, he isn't breathing. But his blood flow apparently changes. His blood changes direction and moves toward his brain and heart to protect them. That apparently keeps these organs from being damaged.

There are lots of interesting people in *Gaia Symphony*. Another one is Reinhold Messner, who has climbed every 8,000-meter peak in the world without an oxygen tank. When they asked him how he did it, he said the same kind of thing: "I become the mountain," or, "After I become the mountain, I can climb it." When they asked him what it feels like to stand on top of a mountain, he said he becomes the top. So it's perfectly natural that he can survive in those conditions despite the lack of oxygen.

Mayol and Messner are essentially saying the same thing. But what's interesting is that, although both of them experience the exact same thing, one climbs mountains and the other dives into the sea – one only thinks about diving and the other only thinks about climbing.

We all have to live our lives according to what's most important to us. But the way we express this and the way we live varies from one person to the next. This is where individuality comes into play. In the process of living, we actualize our individuality.

You could argue that the fundamental human condition is to some degree universal, but as we live within this universality, our individuality inevitably emerges. For some people, the only choice is to dive into the sea, others are compelled to climb mountains, and still others can do nothing but write novels.

Murakami: *Or become psychotherapists.*

Kawai: Exactly. I believe that I had no choice but to do what I'm doing. That's what makes it interesting.

Murakami: *That brings me to my next question. Both of our jobs can be classified as social acts, but what about people who aren't so lucky?*

Kawai: You have to feel sorry for people like that. Take, for example, someone who believes that they will be healed by killing someone. That's a truly pitiful thing. Our job as therapists is to meet people like this, and together to try and come up with a way for them to express themselves in order to somehow be accepted in society – or to take the symbolic truth of murder and convert it into a socially acceptable form.

Kawai: People Who Are Healed by Killing

This is a very heavy subject, but it's something that can't be avoided in psychotherapy. Killing should be seen as including an element of killing oneself or committing suicide. The only way that the person can go on living is to kill someone or kill themself.

There are people like this. But this is a 'truth' that is strictly limited to that person and we cannot draw any general rules or conclusions from it. Some might say I'm overly optimistic, but as a psychotherapist, I do everything in my power to help people who are burdened with this type of fate to survive in the world by creating some kind of 'story.'

Some people experience murder or suicide in their dreams. When this is accompanied by a strong emotional reaction, they seem to experience healing through the act

119

In that sense, the work we do relies on a different standard of right and wrong. Generally, if someone said they wanted to die, you would try to talk them out of it, or if a child refused to go school, you'd try to convince them to go. But a therapist would probably say something like, "Going to school is fine, and not going is also fine" or, "Dying isn't such a bad thing." Otherwise, we wouldn't be able to deal with them.

Here's another example. Some mental health specialists become too lax. When someone like this presents a case that they have diagnosed at an academic meeting, people become deeply annoyed and weary. And after the presentation is finished, the audience (made up of other professionals in

---

of killing. I have died many times in my clients' dreams – despite stubbornly surviving in real life. By confronting the symbolical reality of 'killing,' I have done all I possibly can to deal with those who can only be healed by 'killing.'

It seems to me that in literature, suicide and murder have a similar sort of meaning.

After one treatment was over, the client said, "The most unfortunate thing about meeting you was that I wasn't able to kill myself." This is a very vague expression, but you might interpret it to mean that the person, who could have been healed by suicide, chose to go on living in this world by deliberately opting for an 'unhealed' life after meeting me. This comment stuck with me, and on occasion it comes to mind as I reflect on the state of my practice.

At any rate, one thing it is impossible to make generalizations about is death.

the field) confronts the person with very aggressive questions.

But when a reputable person does the same thing, though it might defy common sense, it seems perfectly reasonable. In that case, people don't feel annoyed or weary. It's very hard to say exactly where the line between the two is. And in the same way, it's difficult to simply say that you shouldn't kill someone.

Still, the important thing is that there's some kind of clear line. Without that, both the patient and I would go crazy. Or maybe I wouldn't go crazy, but the patient would.

Murakami: *People Who Are Healed by Killing*

There really are people like this who are healed by killing – people who could not be healed by anything else... I translated Shot in the Heart, *a story(-like) book about the American serial killer Gary Gilmore, and he was a perfect example. The writer (Gilmore's younger brother) traced, recorded, and verified the chain of events that led Gilmore to become a killer back to the family's ancestors some 150 years ago. The book is so persuasive that you can't help but ruminate on the idea that the human heart is relentlessly pursued by these distant connections. It's an incredible book.*

Gilmore had descended into a deep state of despair about his life, and in that period when the death penalty was in the midst of being abolished in America, he defied public opinion and chose to be executed by a firing squad. I think translating this book greatly altered my perception of human beings.

19. Religion and Psychotherapy

Murakami: *It seems to me that in terms of this standard of right and wrong, [Aum Shinrikyo leader] Shoko Asahara was quite sick. Is it possible to cure someone like that?*

Kawai: It depends on the person.

When you get right down to it, it's a question of stature. If I have a higher stature than him, I can deal with him, but if it's the other way around, it won't work. It's really like a contest between two people. And another amazing thing is, if a child of six had a higher stature than me, I would lose.

Murakami: *By that do you mean that it's very difficult for a religious person or a psychotherapist or psychoanalyst to succeed?*

Kawai: Yes, very difficult. But psychoanalysts are protected by science, and since they consider certain things to be abnormal and prescribe specific medications, it's a bit different from our way of working.

In a way, our approach is similar to a religious person except that we don't have any dogma. We would never say something like, "Chant the name of Buddha and you will be saved." Instead, we have a high regard for what each person discovers on their own. Then we help them consider whether it is possible for this discovery to coexist with contemporary society. That's why we learn so much from them – we really do.

Asahara's trial is currently underway, so the problem of his actions is essentially being dealt with as a social problem – in other words, it is a question related to the legal or social system. It would be pointless to clumsily intervene in the situation; the only thing you can do is let society take care of things. It is, however, a very difficult situation for Aum believers.

Murakami: *It's as if they're bound by a kind of code and until someone deciphers it, nothing will emerge.*

Kawai: Exactly. The people who joined the group were all hoping to be saved in one way or another. That's why simply demanding that they leave the group won't work; you have to offer them something else that will save them in return.

Murakami: *Do you have patients in a similar kind of situation?*

Kawai: Yes. If they came to me, I would treat them. But it's not the kind of thing where I would stretch my hand out to them. And as far as the religions we deal with, they involve all kinds of crazy things. Some of them jump into fires, and others run across swords.

People with problems just happen to run into people from these groups. They find them standing at the foot of a bridge and say, "Oh, you look like you're in trouble." The troubled person is stunned by this and they quickly agree to go with the person. The religious person says something like, "I would like to show you an example of divine power," and they run through fire. Then the troubled person is immediately hooked.

When the person comes back to see me, they say, "Thanks for your help, Doctor. I didn't really get anything out of coming to see you, but I found someone to save me." When I hear this, I understand immediately what's going on, so I say, "Well, I know it's very tough, but why don't come and see me a little bit more?" But once they've gone over to the religious group, there's nothing you can do but let them go. Then I say, "Just remember that if you ever want to come back, you're always welcome."

Typically, after they join a group like that, they experience all kinds of crazy things and that really does heal them to a certain extent. But after all of those crazy experiences, it becomes very difficult for them to return to the real world, because the real world is so full of common sense. That's when they come back to see me. They tell me about joining the group and what they experienced, and I say, "Is that right?" I listen to their story, and try to help them return to this world. But you have to be very careful. When they say that they're going to join a group like that, it's really a matter of life and death, and that's extremely worrying to me. The other thing that worries me is the question of money. That's something you have to be very, very careful about. I always ask them how much money they have to give to the group.

20. The Khalkhyn Gol Incident

Murakami: *In my novels, I often write about paranormal phenomena or surrealistic things, but in
real life I don't really believe in that kind of thing.
I wouldn't completely rule them out, but I basically
don't believe they exist. In fact, I don't give them
much thought.*

*But recently I had a very strange experience. I
went to Khalkhyn Gol [the Khalakh River in Mon-
golia], and I asked someone from the Mongolian
army to show me the ruins of the battlefield there.
Out there in the middle of the desert in a place that
few people have ever visited, everything was exactly
like it was during the war. There were tanks, artillery
shells, canteens, and it looked like the war had just
ended the other day. I was astounded. The air is dry
there, so nothing has rusted. And it's so remote that
it would be too expensive to turn everything into
scrap metal, so they just left it there.*

*I picked up some fragments of a mortar shell and
a bullet as a kind of memorial to the fallen soldiers.*

Then I made the long, half day or so, trip back to town. When I put the objects in my hotel room, I felt repelled by them because they seemed so graphic.

Then I suddenly woke up in the middle of the night and the room was shaking violently. But I was completely awake. It was shaking so violently that it was almost impossible to walk, so at first I thought it was an earthquake. Then I crawled through the darkness, opened the door, and went outside, but everything was completely silent. I had no idea what had happened. At first, I thought it was because I had tapped into a particular mental wavelength – it was as if I had committed myself too strongly to Khalkhyn Gol in my story. Rather than a paranormal event, it seemed somehow connected to my work.

The Khalkhyn Gol Incident

In our daily lives, we almost never come face to face with death, but as I stood on the battlefield in Khalkhyn Gol, the site of a ferocious conflict, there was almost nothing except death. I could distinctly feel it. That was the first time I had experienced anything like this. The war and the deaths occurred there nearly 60 years ago, but vivid signs of death still pervade that small corner of the desert. I'm not saying there were spirits wafting through the air or anything like that; I mean that I perceived something there that closely corresponded to death. It was impossible for me to see that as part of the distant past or someone else's concerns. I had the vague feeling that my eerie experience in the middle of the night at the hotel and the resulting emotional jolt were caused by that.

Kawai: It's very difficult to give things like this a name, but I know that they do happen.

I would simply say that they exist without trying to provide a poor explanation for them – it would just be pseudoscientific to do that. In pseudoscience, you could try to explain the event by saying that the mortar fragments contained some kind of energy.

When you consult with a patient as a therapist, you try to take everything into consideration: "Does it rain whenever I meet this person?" "Does it just happen to be windy today?"

Basically, it's impossible to cure the people that come to see me using ordinary common sense. It's vital for me to remain open to every possibility, and in that realm, I would say that it is possible for the kind of thing you described to occur.

Murakami: *I never have any dreams...*

Kawai: That's because you write novels. [The poet] Shuntaro Tanigawa told me the same thing – he said he almost never dreams. I said, "Of course, you don't – you write poetry."

Murakami: *If you don't have dreams, do they surface in some other form?*

Kawai: I think dreaming becomes difficult – especially when you're writing a story like, *The Wind-Up Bird Chronicle* – because your real life and your writing are taking place completely parallel to each other. So there isn't any need to dream. And if you tried to force yourself to dream on top of your writing, it would cause something terrible to happen.

Murakami: *My wife is constantly having dreams.*

Kawai: It makes perfect sense that she would.

Murakami: *I only have one dream. I always dream I'm levitating in the air, but I'm actually just floating a little bit off the ground. It's a very pleasant feeling. I know precisely what I need to do to get up there. So if you asked me to float right now, I think I really could.*

Kawai: Levitating in midair is basically storytelling – you're just floating up a little bit, right? Only children dream of suddenly soaring way up into the sky – adults never do.

Kawai: Paranormal Phenomena

Though not everything that is referred to as a paranormal phenomenon is true, some of these things certainly are. However, many of them are true on a one-time-only basis and only for that particular person.

In many cases, when a person who experienced such a thing recounts what happened to them, they are met with disbelief or ignored. In order to convey to people what occurred inside of you due to the experience, (rather than the experience itself), it is necessary to rely on a story.

In that sense, you might see the things that happened to Murakami in Khalkhyn Gol as a formative experience for the story in *The Wind-Up Bird Chronicle*.

Also, it's quite common for dreams and reality to coincide. And some of the things that coincide in our dreams are very certain.

Murakami: *Huh, what do you mean?*

Kawai: They contain a sense of certainty. Let's say you had a dream in which person X died. In the dream, you might think, "Oh no, X died." Then when you wake up, you still have the lingering feeling that X is dead, and as it turns out, he really is.

On the other hand, let's say you had a dream in which person Y died, and you merely thought, "Oh no, I dreamed that that guy died," and didn't think any more about it. In cases like that, Y usually isn't really dead. A lot of people would say, "That's absurd!" But in a real situation where, for example, we ask someone in the train to keep an eye on our bag for a minute, we approach someone who looks dependable. Even though we've never seen them before, for some reason or other, we decide that the person is okay, and this almost never proves to be wrong. On rare occasions, something does go wrong, though, and when we come back, our bag is gone.

In other words, based on our life experiences, we quickly make an overall judgment in each particular situation. With practice, I think it's possible to do the same thing in your dreams. That's why I'm also practicing.

When you have a sense of certainty, even when it's not in a dream, you sometimes think, "Oh, that person must be in some kind of danger." Since there is no real basis for this and it's better not to verbalize this feeling, we only think about it. But later we sometimes think that we should have actually said something. If we said things like, "Whatever you do, don't get on that train tomorrow!", every time we felt like that, we'd go absolutely nuts. But if you gradually develop your sense of certainty, it's likely that the probability will increase. I believe that this kind of thing is possible.

People have been doing the same thing as far back as Murasaki Shikibu's time.

Murakami: *I'm writing all of the time and don't usually give it much thought, but sometimes I feel the power of the dead very strongly. Writing a novel is very similar to going down into the netherworld. Sometimes when I write, I suddenly have the feeling that I am anticipating my own death.*

Kawai: Human beings suffer from all kinds of illnesses, but the most fundamental illness is that we die. Other animals are probably not aware of this fact, but human beings come to realize it very early on, and we are forced to incorporate death into our view of life. In a way, this means that we are ill.

People who are able to forget this might be able to live without anything resembling an illness, but the fact is, death remains a constant concern for us.

There are many different methods of dealing with this, but one that seems very effective to me is investigating the place that you are most likely to go after you die. By going down and visiting the netherworld a few times, you gradually come to understand how to get there and where you're going.

The modern and contemporary eras have been very unusual in that there was such a strong focus on living while thinking as little as possible about dying. This is because scientific and technological developments have expanded the potential for human life so rapidly. In this environment, it's difficult to think much about death. But in recent years, people have begun to feel that simply accepting these developments doesn't necessarily lead to happiness. This has led to a sudden urge to discuss death.

If you are seriously considering human beings, it is inevitable that you must also consider death. In that sense, this is something that has been going on constantly since the stories of the Heian Period.

21. Violence and Expression

Murakami: *Something else related to the issue of physicality is violence, which is a big problem. This played a big part in* The Wind-Up Bird Chronicle.

When I wrote my first novel, Hear the Wind Sing, *I made it a kind of rule that I would not write about death or sex. This was based on the fact that modern literature had dealt with these subjects in such a logical manner.*

For example, when I was in my teens, [the novelist] Kenzaburo Oe was a star. He wrote about sex, death, and violence in a very subjective manner. When I started writing in the '80s, I wanted to do something different.

In the end, though, that seemed like the only direction to go, so in Norwegian Wood, *which I wrote ten years later, all I wrote about was sex and death. Of course, my way of writing was different from Oe's and at that point, there was still no violence in my books.*

Then five or six years later, I finally started writing about violence. I'm not sure why. Jay Rubin, who did the English translation of The Wind-Up Bird Chronicle, *went so far as to ask me why I had included such terribly violent scenes. He suggested that it was a betrayal of the reader's trust, because the protagonist seems like a nice person and the reader sympathizes with him, so no matter how bad the other character happens to be, it doesn't seem right for the protagonist to crack his head open with a baseball bat. I couldn't provide him with a good explanation.*

Kawai: I think it is even more meaningful for a character that the reader identifies and sympathizes with to be so deeply involved with violence.

This means that he also has a violent side. And this is something that all of us have.

If human beings didn't have the ability to use

Murakami: *The Difference between Violence in the '60s and Violence Today*

When you think about it, the '60s were a strange time because 'peace and love' and violence existed at the same time, and both of them had a strong influence on us. At the time, that seemed like a perfectly regular thing... But when you think about it, peace and love was an ideal state, and it provided a foundation for the fierce resistance and conflict with everything else. It was very much like the last scene in Easy Rider. *Of course, they were destined to be crushed by the powers that be. During that period, we could clearly detect the smell of the adrenalin that triggered violence, but now that's gone and all that's left are memories.*

violence or brute force, they wouldn't be able to survive. That's true of everything – be it hunting, gathering, or farming.

Not only that, but human beings form communities, and when they decide to invade another area, it wouldn't be possible without violence.

In Western countries, violence is incorporated in the rules. In other words, even when it comes to something like war, as long as it's a fair war, it's okay. This is also true of all kinds of sports.

Murakami: *That means that, for example, violence based on Christianity is okay.*

Kawai: Yes. In Japan, it's pretty difficult to make a rule like that, but we've somehow managed to coexist.

In Japan's case, the truly unfortunate thing is that because of that big war, there has been an

---

Much of the violence in the '60s was used in conflicts and acts of resistance. Regardless of whether it was right or not, it definitely had an easily understandable aesthetic quality. At the time [the novelist Kenzaburo] Oe wrote a lot of stories about that kind of violence and the smell of adrenaline drew many young readers to his work. But it's not like that anymore. Many of the wars that occurred after the end of the Cold War have been marked by local fighting and sectarianism without an overriding sense of direction. The smell of adrenaline has been diffused. I think there is a need to incorporate this new kind of violence into a narrative form. Rather than trying to explain how it is in words, we have to express it in stories.

extreme rejection of violence. Based on the notion that peace is important, there was a total ban placed on children playing army and sword fighting. In other words, they have grown up without ever experiencing their own violent impulses.

That's why they suddenly go wild when they hit puberty and want to do something crazy like bullying other kids. Bullying has been around forever, so bullying in itself isn't something we should be afraid of. It has always existed throughout the world and throughout history. The problem lies in the fact that bullying sometimes leads to killing.

As it seems to me, one reason for this is that when children are small, they never have a chance to experience violence. People tell them they shouldn't do things like kill insects. When I was a child many years ago, in the process of killing frogs or whatever it was, we suddenly came to the realization that it wasn't good to kill animals. Anyway, contemporary Japanese people have become bizarrely preoccupied with peace and we have deeply repressed our feelings related to violence in order to create a divide between the body and the mind. I think this also explains the sudden outbreak of violence in works of art. Not long before this era, which is sometimes called the 'Age of Peace,' all kinds of crazy things were going on. I think that Japanese culture and contemporary Japan are shouldering a tremendous subconscious burden. At some point something has to give – and we should all be aware of that.

22. Violence in Japanese Society

Murakami: *One of the motifs in* The Wind-Up Bird Chronicle *is trying to bring Kumiko back. She has been dragged into a world of darkness. To bring her back from that world, it is necessary to use violence. Without violence, getting her back would not trigger a catharsis or have any persuasive power.*

Until I wrote that part, I hadn't given any particular thought to depicting violence, but in order to bring her back into the world of light, there was a need for something with that kind of impact. It was necessary to turn things around *through some form of violence.*

Another reason was that the world of darkness contains an endless accumulation of violence from throughout history. For example, at the end of the first part, there's a flaying scene, but I don't really know why I wrote about that subject. Then there's the Chinese massacre scene. That was something else I didn't completely understand, but I decided to write about it.

Finally, at the end of the third part, the violence used to bring Kumiko back from the world of darkness functions as a response to that historical violence or a kind of probability.

It wasn't until later, after I read the text and started to think about it, that I realized it was my way of making sense of history.

Kawai: When you think about it, [Tokyo] Governor Yukio Aoshima's decision to cancel the World City Expo was a very violent act. It was also the result of many different things that had accumulated up until that point. I think that kind of violence is

---

Kawai: On Violence

Murakami's suggestion that the violence in the third volume of *The Wind-Up Bird Chronicle* is a kind of probability that functions as a response to historical violence is extremely important. Japanese people should make an effort to become conscious of the violence within them and discover an appropriate way of expressing it. Unless they do this, we are likely to see an increasing number of incidents in which assailants break out in an uncontrollable rage. The Aum incident is one example. Another manifestation of modern violence is when perfectly innocent people are infected with the HIV virus in the process of receiving some kind of medical treatment.

Whether it's Aum or HIV-infected blood products, the original motivation for these things was not at all violent. On the contrary, it was rooted in the desire to do something 'right' or 'good.' But this contains the potential for something very dangerous and violent to occur. To avoid this, it is necessary to recognize the violence within yourself from the outset and act accordingly.

necessary today. If you get rid of all of the violence and everyone just keeps talking about peace, I think it will eventually have the opposite effect and lead to chaos.

Murakami: *Ultimately, Japan's biggest problem is that the war ended, and we never had an opportunity to process the overwhelming violence that occurred during the war. Everyone acted like they were victims, and their real feelings were replaced with extremely ambiguous phrases like, "We must never repeat this mistake again." No one ever took any personal responsibility for the mechanism that created the violence.*

Murakami: *The Age of Conflict*

Many things have been said about the significance of this Age of Unrest, but in the end, we had the fundamentally optimistic idea that, "we wanted to make the world a better place," and we made a sincere effort to implement this idea. At that time, we knew exactly what was bad and what was good, and simply believed that by destroying something bad, something good would emerge. Everything was very black and white – for example, John Lennon was good and Richard Nixon was bad. So there's absolutely no reason why ordinary physical violence wouldn't somehow be involved.

Of course, this was nothing more than a 'story.' But we basically believed that story and saw it as part of the postwar flow of time. In other words, the social narrative was directly linked to the personal narrative. And we were provided with a temporary field of activity.

Ultimately, however, this story was merely what we saw as the postwar establishment from our side. On the other side, I imagine there was a much more solemn and larger field, which as Kawai suggests, was rooted in Japanese cultural patterns.

I think the problems of my generation are also rooted in this. My generation, which grew up with the 'Pacifist Constitution,' was raised on three principles: "Peace is everything," "Never repeat the same mistake again," and "Abolish war." When we were children, that was okay – these things in themselves are admirable notions. But as we grew up, we discovered endless contradictions and discrepancies. That's what led to the riots in 1968 and '69. Yet, everything just continued on and on, without ever reaching a resolution.

Kawai: As I see it, young people at that time did not acknowledge the violence within themselves. They simply thought that what they were doing was right, so they did it. But because they didn't go beyond that and gain an awareness of the violent impulses at work, their efforts were doomed to fail.

If your goal is to destroy cultural patterns that Japanese people have followed for many years, it's necessary to use violence – in various senses of

---

Kawai: *The Age of Conflict*

It is deeply unfortunate that the movement ended without producing any plausible results, because the students were unaware of how 'Japanese' the things they were doing were. At the time, I often talked, somewhat jokingly, about how great it would be if the government used even half of its budget to resolve the conflict by giving the main students who were involved in these activities an opportunity to study abroad.

the word. But since young people were operating within the same cultural patterns, there was no way to destroy them. They used an extremely simple, primitive form of violence, so it was all over by the time the riot squad arrived.

Murakami: *Right. In terms of their ability to wage violence, the police are pros.*

Ultimately, I think the reason it took me so long to deal with violence in my writing was that I had to come to terms with all of those ambiguities.

From here on out, my mission is to figure out a way of dealing with the violence that is necessary to strike a balance in history. I have the feeling that that's part of my generational responsibility.

Kawai: That's true. If young people today become aware enough to deal with the problem of how to express violence, that would be fine, but…

Murakami: *I have a very strong feeling that another age of violence is on the way. And when it arrives, the real question is, what kind of values are going to be attributed to violence?*

Do you have the sense that Japanese society is degenerating?

Kawai: It depends on your point of view, but in a sense almost nothing has changed. Social and cultural movements occur at a very slow pace.

23. Pain and Nature

Murakami: *I've always thought that it was good to have all kinds of sex-related businesses. Maybe 'good' isn't the right word – natural? Whatever people want to do, they should be able to do – it doesn't have anything to do with right or wrong. For instance, some people get angry because young people today don't have any guts. Regardless of whether this is true or not, it isn't a question of right and wrong; it's just the way things are. It's not as if young people chose to be that way, so it's impossible to see it in terms of a standard of good or bad.*

In that sense, I'm not interested in judging things that are happening in society as a critic. As a novelist, however, I do feel I have a responsibility in regard to the way I process my feelings.

For example, there is really a sense of violence in the air at the moment. But when it comes to figuring out how to process this, over and above the question of whether it is right or wrong, and considering what I can do about it, everything becomes very difficult.

Kawai: The people who really have the power to systematize this kind of thing are called politicians. They create structures that lead to legitimate social power. To give a very bad example, Hitler was someone who was amazingly good at this.

Murakami: *When I look at Japanese society, I think that righteousness without pain or hardship is not righteousness. For instance, everyone opposes France's nuclear tests. What they're saying is undoubtedly correct, but no one is feeling any pain. An anti-nuclear declaration was issued by a group of writers. As a protest, that's certainly the correct response, but in the sense that no one is ultimately experiencing any pain in the world context, it is a mistake.*

In that sense, Ryu Murakami is a very astute writer. From the very beginning, he clearly foresaw the violence and wrote about it. In my case, it took much longer to get to that point, and his approach to society is also different from mine.

Are you also aware of this sense of violence in contemporary society?

Kawai: Definitely. In fact, I sometimes commit little acts of violence myself.

Murakami: *You mean like telling lies? (laughs)*

Kawai: You might say I'm still putting up a futile resistance or struggling against a formidable opponent. I keep thinking I'd like to resort to 'violence' – but not actual violence. Unless you make skillful use of violence, it's not interesting.

Murakami: *No One Is Feeling Any Pain*

The idea that no one is feeling any pain is probably an exaggeration on my part. There were undoubtedly some people who did and I'm in no position to draw this type of conclusion. But I still think the majority of people haven't dealt with the pain…

In my case at least, I thought, "At this point, I can't find a good way of dealing with the pain," which made it impossible to commit myself to this type of action. I wouldn't completely rule out the idea that this has to do with my excessive self-consciousness. But I find it impossible to simply accept a movement on the basis of a certain thing being correct, and therefore good, and something else being incorrect, and therefore bad. I can only see things in terms of what I myself feel is right. Without a strong sense of conviction, it's hard to simply take action – even when you spend a long time thinking about it. I can never really bring myself to believe the idea that "everything is meaningless unless you take action." This might be because of what I learned firsthand as a university student.

24. Where Are We Headed?

Murakami: *I dealt with the Khalkhyn Gol Incident extensively in my novel, and I've given a lot of thought to why I chose that subject.*

I read all kinds of things about the incident and I began to wonder, "Assuming I was as logical and stable as I am now, how long would I be able to take it, if by some twist of fate I was thrown into a place like that?" It was a very frightening thing to consider.

The most impressive thing I read about Khalkhyn Gol had to do with the chaotic state of the Japanese army. By rights, the military should have been very systematic, but it was actually very chaotic. That seemed very frightening.

The last time we met*, you talked about flexibility being one of the merits of the Japanese system and

---

*The "last time we met" refers to a public dialogue between the two that was held at Princeton University in 1994. A transcript of the event can be found in *Listening to the Voice of the Heart: A Collection of Discussions with Hayao Kawai* (Shincho Bunko).

the antithesis of Western consistency. I completely understand this now, and since I've returned to Japan, I am in a situation in which, for better or worse, I have to operate within this system. At the same time, however, I have a certain amount of fear in regard to this flexible structure. The way I resolve this feeling is an important theme for me. What are your thoughts on this subject?

Kawai: That structure will never change without a great deal of violence. But the power of the pen is one form of violence.

Murakami: *But the pen is virtually powerless against the dynamic violence of the state. For example, a writer can't effectively do anything to resist war.*

Kawai: Even so, you have to try. You have no choice but to do whatever you can.

Murakami: *But Japanese society is more emotional than logical.*

Kawai: That's certainly true.

Murakami: *Does that make it easier to operate?*

Kawai: Yes, if you can manage the situation.

Murakami: *Today, more than ever, we as a society don't seem to know where we're headed. This is because we haven't properly dealt with the past. We*

*moved into the economic sphere based on the logic of
"never repeating the same mistake again."*

*We've been economically active for many years,
we've grown rich, we've turned into an export-based
nation, and right now we're faced with the Gulf War.
If we were a small, agricultural country, no one
would say a word about our decision not to dispatch
armed forces. But since Japan has made its name
as an industrial nation and emerged victorious in
the global economic sphere, it seems logical to the
rest of the world that we would respond positively
to a request for military support. So now we find
ourselves in the midst of a contradiction.*

Kawai: Yes, and when you get right down to it, you
might also argue that Japanese people don't have
any right to oppose the French nuclear tests.

Murakami: *Under the circumstances, we must now
make a policy decision to determine where we are
headed. I see this as an extremely urgent matter.*

Thinking back on The Wind-Up Bird Chronicle
*now, I am slowly starting to make sense of it. First, I
came to my own personal understanding of historical violence, and now I'm at a point where I have to
figure out which direction I should go in next. But I
don't know exactly where this will lead me.*

*I do feel, however, that in doing this, I will be
forced to think very careful about morality. This*

reminds me of what you said earlier about that invisible line.

Kawai: It is extremely difficult to verbalize the type of morality you're talking about.

Murakami: *But isn't verbalizing it one of the problems that we have to face?*

Kawai: Yes, it's something that we must confront head on. I see that as one of our duties.

Murakami: *In practical terms, though, you have cured many people by drawing a clear distinction between things that can't be verbalized.*

Kawai: Yes, that's right. Except in my case, that has a lot of do with personal experience. We refer to what we do as curing, but in a way it's the opposite of ordinary life. It's not as if I'm trying to uphold any moral principles. As the person sitting in front of me comes up with things that are intrinsically meaningful, we very gradually arrive at certain distinctions. I also believe that by doing as much as I possibly can for a person, I no longer have to consider the world as a whole. In the end, seriously ill people are suffering from the world's illnesses. That's what I would like to tell our society. But my statements are based entirely on the individual. I keep an eye on statistics and world developments, but everything I say stems from the individual.

Murakami: *Do you think that at some point you might take on a few apprentices (kind of like a religious figure), and share some rules of thumb with them?*

Kawai: No, I don't think so. If you're not careful, that kind of thing can become very dangerous. Thinking about something like that would cause that dynamic line to disappear, and I have made a conscious decision not to accept any apprentices on an individual basis.

Murakami: *In other words, your experiences will remain with you until the end?*

Kawai: Yes, but my basic stance is to convey whatever I have learned. I'm still not sure. As I get a little older, I might start talking about apprentices and things. (laughs) Human beings are weak creatures.

Afterword

You often hear older people bemoaning the fact that today's youth are dispirited and university students are too docile. It certainly does seem that way. But this is not to say that there has been an abrupt decline in the quality of young people in the contemporary era. It's simply that the image we once had of the 'rebellious youth' is no longer applicable.

It's difficult to grasp the type of burden that hangs over today's young people, and at present, they are in no position to express themselves through resistance. Seeing the deep anguish ('anguish' doesn't begin to convey what they're feeling) the young people in the consolation room are suffering, I sometimes wonder if I have what it takes to be of any real use to them.

I first came to Haruki Murakami's novels on the recommendation of someone who came to see me. I'm not much of a reader, but sometimes in connection to my job as a psychotherapist, I come across an unexpectedly interesting book. Of all Murakami's books, I was most drawn to *A*

Wild Sheep Chase. The character of the Sheep Man is a brilliant embodiment of the mental state that today's young people are struggling with.

As I read the book, I was instantly reminded of Soseki Natsume's novel, *Sanshiro*, a favorite of mine when I was in university. Perhaps the life of the main character, who moves to Tokyo from the country, overlapped with my own life, as someone who moved from Tanba Sasayama, the epitome of country, to Kyoto. By comparing the 'stray sheep' that Sanshiro encounters in Natsume's book with Murakami's Sheep Man, I realized just how much the world has changed. In fact, comparing the two books became so interesting that I later wrote about it in *Youthful Dreams and Play* (Iwanami Shoten Publishers). I'll omit that discussion here, though.

As I was reading Murakami's books one after another, the first two volumes of *The Wind-Up Bird Chronicle* arrived. I had the sense that this book was of a higher order than his previous works. First of all, he had moved away from the subject of youth and was dealing with contemporary people at large. Also, the book was closely aligned with 'healing through stories.' This was an idea I had come up with some time back, but I had only recently written about it.

For two months in the spring of 1994, I was at Princeton University in the U.S. Murakami had already moved from Princeton to Boston, but he made a special trip back to Princeton to meet me. The goal was to conduct a public discussion (arranged by the Shinchosha Publishing Company), primarily related to *The Wind-Up Bird Chronicle*.

Since my specialty is clinical psychology, I was interested and happy to meet a new person, but I'm still innately shy around strangers and I do whatever I can to avoid meeting anyone new. I tend to annoy editors by just listening and agreeing without offering my own opinion. A lot of people see this as modesty, but that doesn't really have anything to do with it – for some reason, all of my ideas just seem to vanish in these situations. In Murakami's case, it was different. I babbled on and on about my thoughts (and some things I hadn't even thought about!). When I thought back on it, it seemed as if I had talked incessantly for two whole days. We got along extremely well.

As a result, I was delighted to take part in this project. The third volume of *The Wind-Up Bird Chronicle* had also just come out, so I had all kinds of things I wanted to say. You already know the title of this book, but if it had been up to me, I would have called it, *Hayao Kawai Wanted to Meet Haruki Murakami*.

The two of us have some similar ideas, but since we belong to different generations, Murakami is much more deeply immersed in American culture than I am, and he has a fresh awareness about everything. As someone living in the contemporary era, I've made a conscious effort to evolve, but

I'm still deeply rooted in the Japanese soil and give off a rustic scent. Murakami's astute questions led to some unexpected twists and talking with him was very enjoyable.

Japan has arrived at a difficult point in its history. In the past, we deftly skimmed off the top layer of Western culture, but I think the time has finally come to confront our roots. This is a perception shared by both Murakami and myself.

As Japanese culture is forced to change, one of the greatest difficulties will be human relations. We are currently wavering between old and new as we decide how to deal with this problem. This is best exemplified by marital relationships. The way that Japanese couples related to each other in the past is no longer valid. And yet, if we follow the American model, we are likely to see the divorce rate skyrocket. There's nothing wrong with divorce per se, but it would be hard to hold up the American model of marriage as exemplary. As we fumble around looking for a new type of marital relationship, a variety of conflicts between couples are starting to arise. This isn't simply a case of one partner or the other being 'wrong.' In many cases, it has do with the fact that one partner blames the other one for being 'wrong.'

More people are coming to see me about their marriages. These are the same kind of people who at one time would have seen out their lives as 'good couples.' To me, it seems as if these people are suffering from an illness of the culture or the age, or even that they are burdened with Japan's current problems.

The fact that the protagonist's wife in *The Wind-Up Bird Chronicle* suddenly vanishes is completely in line with the present situation. In many households, the husband or wife has symbolically vanished. And some people haven't even noticed.

I believe that stories are actually a very important means of curing illness. Today, the problem lies in our inability to present these stories in a way that can be generally understood. Everyone bears responsibility; we must all create our own stories.

As I have mentioned, on the whole Murakami and I are in agreement. Various differences did arise due to our personalities, but we carried on regardless. As an individual, I gained a great deal from this experience. I would like to extend my sincere gratitude to Haruki Murakami. I would also be very pleased if this book proves to be even slightly useful to you in creating your own stories.

Finally, I would like to express my appreciation to Kazumasa Horikiri and Yoshizumi Higuchi, both editors from Iwanami Shoten, for planning and assisting us with this dialogue.

– Hayao Kawai

Hayao Kawai

Dreams, Myths and Fairy Tales in Japan

edited by J. Gerald Donat

The beloved former Japanese Minister of Culture, best-selling author, university professor and Zürich-trained Jungian analyst, Hayao Kawai, presents here one of his rare works in English.
Dreams, Myths and Fairy Tales in Japan addresses Japanese culture insightfully, exploring the depths of the psyche from both Eastern and Western perspectives, an endeavor the author is uniquely suited to undertake. The book is comprised of five lectures orig- inally delivered at the historic

round-table Eranos Conferences in Ascona, Switzerland.
160 pages, illustrated, ISBN 978-3-85630-544-4

The Rock Rabbit and the Rainbow

Laurens van der Post among Friends

Edited by Robert Hinshaw

Authors from around the world have combined their talents in a tribute honoring this outstanding writer, soldier and statesman, a man of his time. Contributors include: Nelson Mandela, Chief Buthalezi, Joseph Henderson, Alan McGlashan, Ian Player, Jean-Marc Pottiez, T.C. Rob- ertson, Aniela Jaffé, Jonathan Stedall, Harry Wilmer, Jo Wheelwright, C.A. Meier, Kathleen Raine and many others. Included are previously unpublished essays and letters by Sir Laurens himself.
393 pages, illustrated
hardbound ISBN 978-3-85630512-3 / paperback ISBN 978-3-85630-540-6

English Titles from Daimon

Eva Pattis Zoja (Ed.) - *Sandplay Therapy*
Laurens van der Post - *The Rock Rabbit and the Rainbow*
Jane Reid - *Jung, My Mother and I: The Analytic Diaries*
of Catharine Rush Cabot
R.M. Rilke - *Duino Elegies*
Miguel Serrano - *C.G. Jung and Hermann Hesse*
Helene Shulman - *Living at the Edge of Chaos*
D. Slattery / G. Slater (Eds.) - *Varieties of Mythic Experience*
David Tacey - *Edge of the Sacred: Jung, Psyche, Earth*
Susan Tiberghien - *Looking for Gold*
Ann Ulanov - *Spiritual Aspects of Clinical Work*
- *Picturing God*
- *The Female Ancestors of Christ*
- *The Wisdom of the Psyche*
- *The Wizards' Gate, Picturing Consciousness*
Ann & Barry Ulanov - *Cinderella and her Sisters*
A. Schweizer / R. Scheizer-Villers - *Stone by Stone: Reflections on Jung*
Eva Wertenschlag-Birkhäuser - *Windows on Eternity:*
The Paintings of Peter Birkhäuser
Harry Wilmer - *How Dreams Help*
- *Quest for Silence*
Luigi Zoja - *Drugs, Addiction and Initiation*
Luigi Zoja & Donald Williams - *Jungian Reflections on September 11*
Jungian Congress Papers - *Jerusalem 1983: Symbolic & Clinical Approaches*
- *Berlin 1986: Archetype of Shadow in a Split World*
- *Paris 1989: Dynamics in Relationship*
- *Chicago 1992: The Transcendent Function*
- *Zürich 1995: Open Questions*
- *Florence 1998: Destruction and Creation*
- *Cambridge 2001*
- *Barcelona 2004: Edges of Experience*
- *Cape Town 2007: Journeys, Encounters*
- *Montreal 2010: Facing Multiplicity*
- *Copenhagen 2013: 100 Years on*

Our books are available from your bookstore or from our distributors:

AtlasBooks
30 Amberwood Parkway
Ashland OH 44805, USA
Phone: 419-281-5100
Fax: 419-281-0200
E-mail: order@atlasbooks.com
www.atlasbooks.com

Gazelle Book Services Ltd.
White Cross Mills, High Town
Lancaster LA1 4XS, UK
Tel: +44(0)152468765
Fax: +44(0)152463232
Email: Sales@gazellebooks.co.uk
www.gazellebooks.co.uk

Daimon Verlag - Hauptstrasse 85 - CH-8840 Einsiedeln - Switzerland
Phone: (41)(55) 412 2266   Fax: (41)(55) 412 2231
Email: info@daimon.ch
Visit our website: **www.daimon.ch** or write for our complete catalog